COMPREHENSIVE AURAL SKILLS

Comprehensive Aural Skills: A Flexible Approach to Rhythm, Melody, and Harmony is a complete suite of material for both performance and dictation, covering the wide range of sight-singing and ear-training skills required for undergraduate courses of study. It is unique in its integrated and comprehensive approach, with three interchangeable modules: Rhythm, Melody, and Harmony. The authors blend musical examples from the common-practice repertory with original examples that are composed to specifically address particular skills and concepts. Each module includes material for classroom performance, self-directed study, and homework assignments.

Features

- **A complete suite of aural skills material:** *Comprehensive Aural Skills* is a combined sight-singing and ear-training textbook, audio, and companion website package.
- **Customizable organization:** Instructors can interchange the modules and choose freely from the set of exercises to tailor the course based on their students' needs and the school's music theory curriculum.
- **Engaging and practical musical examples:** Examples are selected and composed specifically for the pedagogical context of an aural skills classroom.
- **Streamed performances by professional musicians:** Platform-neutral, so students can access and listen to the examples from any desktop, laptop, tablet, or smartphone.
- **Answer keys to dictation exercises:** for students to work independently.
- **Online resources** for students and teachers:

  - Auxiliary modules: Topics not found in the texts, such as diatonic and chromatic sequences, more modulations to distantly related keys, and an introduction to jazz transcriptions.
  - Teachers' guide: Answers for every homework assignment, tips for integrating written theory, strategies on how to effectively teach, and additional examples and homework assignments to use in class.

Justin Merritt is a composer of award-winning concert music. He currently teaches music composition and theory at St. Olaf College.

David Castro teaches music theory and aural skills at St. Olaf College. His research appears in the *Journal of Music Theory Pedagogy* and he is on the editorial board of *Music Theory Pedagogy Online*.

COMPREHENSIVE AURAL SKILLS

A Flexible Approach to Rhythm, Melody, and Harmony

Justin Merritt and David Castro

Routledge
Taylor & Francis Group

NEW YORK AND LONDON

First published 2016
by Routledge
711 Third Avenue, New York, NY 10017

and by Routledge
2 Park Square, Milton Park, Abingdon, Oxon, OX14 4RN

Routledge is an imprint of the Taylor & Francis Group, an informa business

Library of Congress Cataloging in Publication Data
Merritt, Justin Wayne, 1975– author.
  Comprehensive aural skills.
    pages cm
  Includes bibliographical references and index.
  1. Ear training. 2. Sight-singing. 3. Musical dictation.
  I. Castro, David, 1975– author. II. Title.
  MT35.M58 2016
  781.4'2—dc23   2015008743

ISBN: 978-1-138-90070-7 (hbk)
ISBN: 978-1-138-90071-4 (pbk)
ISBN: 978-1-315-68413-0 (ebk)

Typeset in Stone Serif
by Keystroke, Station Road, Codsall, Wolverhampton

Senior Editor: Constance Ditzel
Editorial Assistant: Aurora Montgomery
Production Manager: Mhairi Bennett
Project Manager: Maggie Lindsey-Jones, Keystroke
Marketing Manager: Jessica Plummer
Copy Editor: Diana Chambers
Proofreader: Fiona Wade
Cover Design: Lisa Dynan

CONTENTS

PREFACE

Comprehensive Aural Skills provides a unique and extensive compendium of exercises for the study of rhythm, melody, and harmony. Written theory and aural skills are integrated so that they are mutually reinforcing, resulting in a comprehensive text that can move at the same speed and reinforce the topics found in music theory textbooks for undergraduate music majors. At St. Olaf College, we have spent many years compiling, composing, and recording these exercises as the basis for our teaching of aural skills. We share it with you now because it is the volume we wish we had when we began to teach theory and aural skills. The materials in this book have been assembled with both teachers and students in mind, and constitute a complete and rigorous aural skills program.

Most aural skills texts focus on only one or two of the above areas and are generally intended to function independently from written theory topics. However, for those music programs that wish to (re-)integrate written theory and aural skills so that they are mutually reinforcing (rather than having them mentally siloed by the student), a need has emerged for a comprehensive text that can move at the same speed and reinforce the skills and concepts students learn in the standard 2–4 semester theory sequence for music majors.

The integrated approach has been in place at St. Olaf College for many years now, and this text arose precisely out of our classrooms. We found that then-available texts served one or two of our aural skills needs, but that no single text provided everything that we needed in order to teach our aural skills classes.

Content

This text brings together the elements that we consider necessary for a well-rounded aural skills curriculum.

- Examples run the gamut from simple exercises for beginners to challenging post-tonal materials.
- Melodies for performance include both "found" excerpts (i.e., from the classical repertory, folk, and world musics) and original compositions that were written specifically with the pedagogy of aural skills in mind.
- Harmonic dictation modules include short, simple, homophonic examples; slightly embellished examples that include suspensions, passing tones, etc.; and longer more elaborate examples in a "melody and accompaniment" style. This was very important to us.
- The simple homophonic examples are deeply musical—equally important—meaning that SATB voice leading rules, conventions with regard to metrical placement of certain harmonies, and so on have been strictly observed.

Organization

Rather than combine all our materials into a single continuous progression, which would thereby prescribe an idealized pacing, we have organized *Comprehensive Aural Skills* in three large sections, allowing each instructor to decide just how quickly his or her class should proceed through the rhythm, melody, and harmony modules. Instructors have complete freedom to structure a given semester or an aural skills curriculum in a way that works for them. To that end, we offer sample curricula that give teachers ideas, including the pacing we use in our own classrooms. Of course, each instructor should feel absolutely free to modify them according to the needs of his or her students. The Dictation Keys can be found at the end of the book (from pages 281–384).

Approach

Rhythm

The rhythm portion of *Comprehensive Aural Skills* begins with four modules on simple meters. Modules 5–7 then develop rhythmic reading and dictation skills in compound meters. After completing Module 2, students can either go on to Module 3 or skip to Module 5 in order to begin working in compound meters as early as possible.

Melody

A glance at the Table of Contents shows that Melody Modules 1–5 proceed from the idea that steps are easier to sing than skips, and that skips are best introduced within limited contexts. We have chosen to use the fundamental harmonies of tonic and dominant as the limiting factors in Modules 3 and 4, although it would be just as easy to think of these modules in terms of the scale degrees that can be leapt into and away from. Module 5 proceeds from this latter way of thinking in that it is not beholden to any particular harmony, but is simply about "diatonic skips." This approach allows the instruction of melody and harmony to mutually reinforce one another.

Melody Modules 6–11 introduce and reinforce chromaticism in relation to the diatonic foundation established in Modules 1–5. Modules 12–14 are intended to complement those theory programs that include the study of Impressionism and Post-tonal materials.

Harmony

Harmony Modules 1–6 can be thought of in two ways, both of which are reflected in their titles. First, these modules are designed to introduce harmonies two or three at a time, beginning with tonic and dominant, and adding from there, based on both structural significance and frequency of occurrence in idiomatic harmonic progressions. The other perspective on these modules is that of the characteristic scale degrees and voice leadings that characterize each of these harmonies. This perspective is particularly valuable to students in dictation exercises, where some more easily hear the melodic contours of the individual voices (as opposed to those who are better at tracking chord qualities). Modules 7–15 are more overtly based on harmonic concerns, although the introductory material to each of these modules also includes detailed information on the scale degrees and voice leadings that are characteristic of each harmony in its typical context.

In short, the focus of both melody and harmony in *Comprehensive Aural Skills* is on the perception of scale degrees, and how they can interact in various ways and to various effects. Although we use movable-*do* solfége, the text within each chapter refers to scale degrees using Schenkerian carats: $\hat{1}$, $\hat{2}$, etc. This was both a nod to the importance of scale degree in Schenker's theories and a conveniently neutral way of allowing each teacher to decide which (if any) solmization system to employ.

The Website www.routledge.com/cw/merritt

In addition to the materials provided in this book, teachers and students should also turn to the accompanying website for several reasons.

1. The website is where they will find streaming audio of the examples for dictation practice in this book. These recordings are provided either for in-class use or to enable independent work outside of

class. Rather than provide you with less than satisfactory MIDI recordings, the streaming audio for this book consists entirely of live performances by professional musicians in a studio environment.

2. Instructors will find (password-protected) examples to use for homework, dictation quizzes, and sight-singing exams. Standardized homework templates make creating homework and exams tailored to the speed and difficulty of your classroom easy.

3. Another reason to consult the website is to find further examples for each module in the book, both for performance and for dictation. Indeed, for various reasons some of our favorite examples are on the website, so student and teacher alike would do well to explore that part of it.

4. Finally, students and teachers will find on the *Comprehensive Aural Skills* website auxiliary modules on topics not included in the text, such as diatonic and chromatic sequences, more modulations to distantly related keys, and an introduction to jazz transcription.

Our goal was to make the website attractive, interactive, and easy to use, with a simple flashcard interface and high-quality streaming audio.

How to Use this Book: For Instructors

Text

Comprehensive Aural Skills is organized into three separate sections so that you can choose a pacing that works for your needs. For example, you can choose to start a first-semester aural skills class with rhythm and melody, and to add harmonic dictation after a week or two. Or you can begin all three at the same time. Or you can hold off on rhythm altogether, giving students an entire semester to focus on melodic performance, and melodic and harmonic dictation. With this book the choice is up to you.

You can also determine how to coordinate any modules that cover roughly the same thing. For example, the skills developed in Melody Module 11: Modulation to Distantly Related Keys overlap with those developed in Harmony Module 15: Modulation Using vii°⁷ and the ct°⁷, which may lead you to design your aural skills sequence in such a way that these two modules begin at the same time. On the other hand, you may see value in having students master the singing and dictation of melodies that modulate to distantly related keys *before* going on to similar harmonic modulations. With *CAS*, either strategy can be easily implemented.

In order to help you plan your class or curriculum, several sample syllabi are available on the *CAS* website (www.routledge.com/cw/merritt). These syllabi can be implemented as they are, or modified in any way you see fit, according to your needs and goals.

Within each module there are examples for performance, which can be used in a variety of ways. The two most important ones are in-class sight-reading and individual practice and preparation outside of class. Because the text offers plenty of examples in each module, you can use either of these strategies at will. And in addition to single-line melodies, the melody modules (and a few of the rhythm modules) also include canons and duets, which allow you to address ensemble skills, such as balance, intonation, tempo, dissonance treatment, and so on. Many more examples are available on the website for either in-class or outside practice.

The dictation exercises in each module come in two sections. The first section is a series of open staves that provide a clef, a key signature, a time signature, and a starting note. Regarding the starting note, rhythmic dictations do not include that because pitch is not a factor, and melodic and harmonic dictations give starting notes at first, but those notes are removed over time, requiring the student to recognize both starting scale degrees and the register in which they appear. After the blanks, each module provides answer keys, providing the student with immediate feedback on her work. Remember that a streaming audio recording of every dictation example is available on the *CAS* website, so these exercises can be used both in class and outside of class.

Finally, for your reference, at the end of the book you will find a guide to solmization of both melody and rhythm, and also a glossary of musical terms.

How Can the Online Materials Help?

The website provides materials that you can use to augment the in-class portion of an aural skills class. First, your students have access to streaming recordings of every dictation example, so you can either use these in class or assign them to students as outside practice.

In addition, the website has extra examples for performance and dictation that correspond with each module, giving students even more opportunities to practice these skills.

The website is also home to a collection of resources for instructors. You will find examples that only you have access to, meaning that they will be suitable for use on homework assignments, quizzes, and/or tests. You will also find sample syllabi that you can either adopt or modify, and commentary on modules that can help you teach skills and concepts more effectively.

How to Use this Book: For Students

It sounds simple, but practice, practice, practice. Each module contains examples for performance so you can improve your sight-reading skills and overall accuracy in interpreting musical notation. Remember that while sight-reading is an important skill, it is also important to review examples that you have already gone through before. By reviewing a particular scale degree, rhythmic pattern, or harmony, you are reinforcing that memory, which will improve your ability to recognize it when it occurs again in a different example.

In addition, each module contains many dictation exercises, so you can practice that skill on a daily basis. Because the website gives you access to a recording of every dictation exercise, you don't have to coordinate schedules with a classmate or wait for the next class period to get more practice—you can work independently to reinforce the skills you are supposed to be acquiring through a course in aural skills.

Justin Merritt
David Castro
March 2015

ACKNOWLEDGMENTS

We would first like to thank our students and colleagues for their support and direction in the creation of this book. In particular, we owe deep gratitude to our St. Olaf colleagues Steven Amundson, Reinaldo Moya, Catherine Ramirez, and Catherine Rodland for their patience with early drafts and for their insightful feedback.

CAS recordings would not have been possible without the help of Jeffrey O'Donnell and the generous support of St. Olaf College, which provided us with two Professional Development Grants that financed all of the recordings in this book.

We also extend our sincere thanks to the staff at Routledge for their faith in this project.

Thanks to Jenni Berg for her work on researching melodies. Gratitude to Anna Schoessler for her tireless engraving work. And thanks to Kevin Dalla Santa for his keen editorial eye.

Thanks to the many professional musicians for their musicianship and artistry:

Francesca Anderegg (violin)
Laura Caviani (piano)
Kurt Claussen (saxophone)
Charles Gray (viola)
David Hagedorn (percussion)
Martin Hodel (trumpet)
Connie Martin (double bass)
Kent McWilliams (piano)
Elinor Niemisto (harp)
Paul Ousley (double bass)
Qian Jun (clarinet)
Cathy Rodland (organ)
Joel Salvo (cello)
Ina Selvelieva (piano)
John Snow (oboe)
Geoffrey Weeks (guitar)
Larry Zimmerman (trombone)

The Loring string quartet: Jonathan Magness (violin), Conor O'Brien (violin), David Auerbach (viola), Adrianna O'Brien (cello)

The Copper Street Brass Quintet: Allison Hall (trumpet), Corbin Dillon (trumpet), Tim Bradley (horn), Alex Wolff (trombone), Nick Adragna (tuba)

The Dolce Woodwind Quintet: Nancy Wucherpfennig (flute), Megan Dvorak (oboe), Karen Hansen (clarinet), Ford Campbell (bassoon), and Vicki Wheeler (horn)

Finally, thanks to Faye Merritt and Ronica Castro for their love, patience, and support.

PART 1

Rhythm

MODULE 1

Simple Meters, Duple and Quadruple

The Dictation Keys for Part 1 can be found at the end of the book (pages 283–293)

Introduction

Because they are so common, meters that are grouped into bars containing two or four beats feel "natural" to us and are known as *simple meters*. By *meter* we mean a regularly recurring pattern of strong and weak beats, which is notated using a meter signature and bar lines.

Consider Example 1.1. The first thing to notice is the meter signature (also known as the time signature), which is the two "fours" at the beginning of the line. The top four indicates that in this excerpt beats will be organized into groups of four at a time, as is shown by the bar lines you see after every fourth note. Each grouping of four is one measure (or bar). The bottom four indicates that the quarter-note is acting as the *beat*. Beat can mean a lot of different things when talking about music, but for our purposes it means the fundamental *pulse*, the periodic emphasis that you would perform if you were asked to clap along with the music. Within each measure the beats are counted in ascending order. Counting along with Example 1.1 would go like this: "One, two, three, four, one, two, three, four," etc.

The next thing to notice is the row of symbols that is given above and below the notes. The top row is a series of *accents* on beats 1 and 3. "Accent" can broadly refer to the emphasis given to any particular note by making it a little louder or a little longer than the ones that come before and after it. Our sense of meter is generated in part by a subtle, yet regular pattern of accents, which is part of performing a particular meter, but usually is *not* notated in the fussy way given in Example 1.1; these accents are merely intended to demonstrate the principle that in $\frac{4}{4}$ time, 1 and 3 are both emphasized beats. Although 1 and 3 are both accented, beat 1 alone is known as the *downbeat* and is the stronger of the two, which is shown by the arrows under the staff. Practice Example 1.1, working towards a steady beat (pulse), and trying to project the meter by accenting 1 and 3 appropriately.

When you can produce a reliable pulse that projects a meter you are ready to subdivide beats into smaller units. In simple meters each beat is divided into two equal parts. Reading from left to right, Example 1.2 shows that a whole-note can be divided into two half-notes, that a half-note can be divided into two quarter-notes, that quarter-notes can be divided into two eighth-notes, and that eighth-notes can be divided into two sixteenth-notes. Note that in in this system note values divide into exactly two of the next smallest note value. Note also that four quarter-notes equal the value of a whole-note, that four sixteenth-notes equal the value of a quarter-note, and so on.

1.2 $\mathbf{o} = \mathbf{d} + \mathbf{d}$ $\mathbf{d} = \mathbf{d} + \mathbf{d}$ $\mathbf{d} = \mathbf{\bigr\rvert} + \mathbf{\bigr\rvert}$ $\mathbf{\bigr\rvert} = \mathbf{\bigr\rvert} + \mathbf{\bigr\rvert}$

When the quarter-note gets the beat, as it does in $\frac{4}{4}$ meter, the eighth-note represents the first level of subdivision. When two eighth-notes occupy a beat they are connected to each other by a beam (as in Example 1.3, measure 1, beats 3 and 4). When eighth-notes are divided into sixteenth-notes they are similarly connected, although with two beams instead of just one (as in Example 1.3, mm. 2 and 3). You should be able to perform Example 1.3 with a steady pulse while still projecting the meter.

1.3

In addition to dividing the beat into smaller units, we can also group it into larger units. Two quarter-notes equal one half-note (Example 1.4, m. 2), which will be held through two full beats. You can think of the whole-note (Example 1.4, m. 3) either as two half-notes or as four quarter-notes. The tricky part about longer note values is maintaining a steady pulse, which requires you to have an "internal" beat. (Notice the "C" that stands in place of the meter signature. This is a shorthand version of $\frac{4}{4}$ that is typically referred to as "common time.")

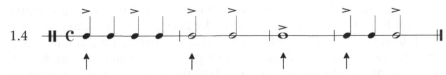

1.4

Example 1.5 shows how dots are used to augment (add to) the value of a given note. The rule of the dot is that it adds half the value of the note it is attached to. Two lines are given in Example 1.5 so you can see how the note *after* the dotted note lines up with a steady stream of quarter-, eighth-, and sixteenth-notes. Notice that when an eighth-note stands alone, it has a flag instead of a beam. Sixteenth-notes are notated similarly, but with two flags. Study Example 1.5 and practice it until you can perform it with a steady beat.

1.5

The last thing to address at the outset is that a particular sequence of note values produces a *rhythm*, which is different from meter because rhythms can change from one beat to the next, and can span several beats. On the other hand, a meter typically remains consistent for a relatively long period of time. We can think of meter as the context and rhythm as the content.

Paradigms

Example 1.6 shows the beat patterns you will encounter in this module, all of which were used in the preceding examples.

1.6

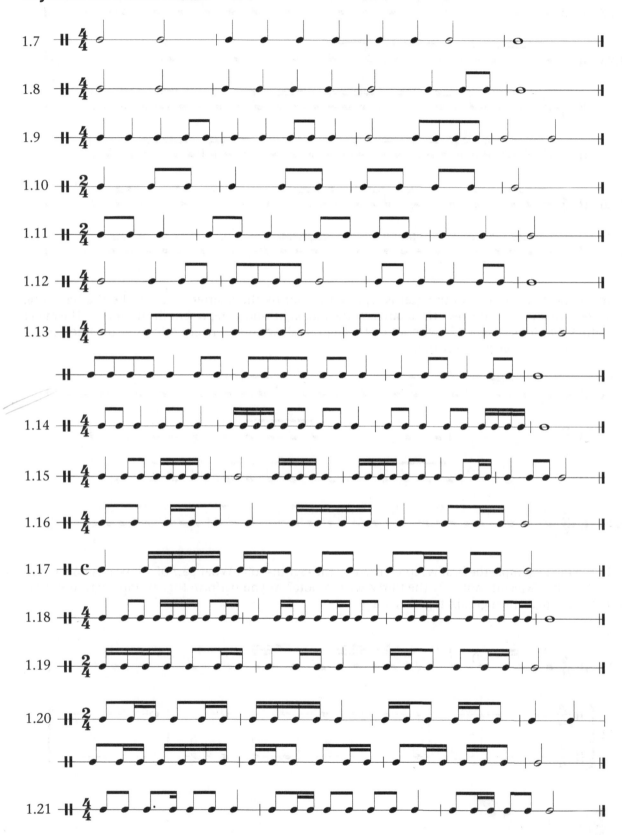

In the next two examples the beat is represented not by the quarter-note, but by the half-note. Consider what parts of the beat the quarter-notes and eighth-notes represent in this meter. The meter signature that looks like a "C" with a line through it is commonly referred to as "Cut time" and is equivalent to a meter signature of $\frac{2}{2}$.

In the next example the beat is represented by the eighth-note. What part of the beat is now represented by the sixteenth-note? By the thirty-second note? As you perform this example pay attention to the beaming, which groups together single beats.

Dictation Practice

1.44 $\Vert$ $\mathbf{4 \atop 4}$ |_____|_____|_____$\Vert$

1.45 $\Vert$ $\mathbf{4 \atop 4}$ |_____|_____|_____$\Vert$

1.46 $\Vert$ $\mathbf{C}$ |_____|_____|_____$\Vert$

1.47 $\Vert$ $\mathbf{2 \atop 2}$ |_____|_____|_____$\Vert$

$\Vert$ |_____|_____$\Vert$

1.48 $\Vert$ $\mathbf{4 \atop 8}$ |_____|_____|_____$\Vert$

1.49 $\Vert$ $\mathbf{2 \atop 4}$ |_____|_____|_____$\Vert$

$\Vert$ |_____|_____|_____$\Vert$

1.50 $\Vert$ $\mathbf{C}$ |_____|_____|_____$\Vert$

$\Vert$ |_____|_____|_____$\Vert$

MODULE 2

Rests and Ties

Introduction

Rests come in the same values as notes and are notated as shown in Example 2.1. Because you don't make any sound during rests it is easy to discount their significance, but silence is one of the most important aspects of music. Be sure to "play" each rest by observing it as an essential part of the rhythmic flow.

2.1

A tie binds two notes together so that the second one is added to the value of the first and is not articulated. For example, the first two measures of Example 2.2 sound identical. A tie can also be used to "cheat" the bar line. For example, in order to begin a half-note on beat 4 of m. 3, it is necessary to tie one quarter-note to another across the bar line because a proper half-note on beat 4 would result in there being 5 beats in that measure. Similarly, the tie into the downbeat of m. 5 creates a note that is equivalent to a dotted quarter-note, but doesn't violate the meter. Finally, ties are used when a note value would otherwise obscure beat 3 in a quadruple meter, as in the last two measures of Example 2.2.

2.2

Rhythms for Performance

2.3

2.4

2.5

2.6

2.7

2.8

The following example contains a dotted rest. Interpret it as you would a note of the same value.

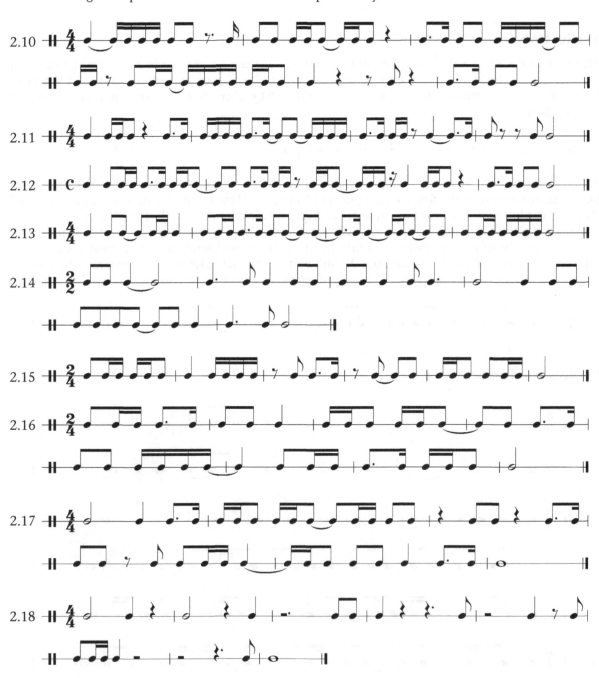

The following example begins with a partial measure, a single quarter-note that leads into the first downbeat. The proper name for an introductory partial measure is *anacrusis*, although it is commonly referred to as a "pick-up."

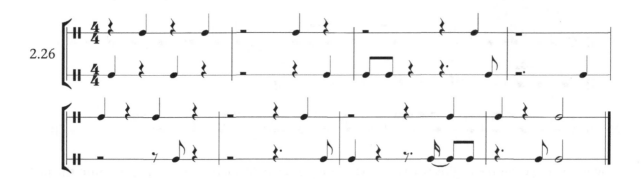

2.26

Dictation Practice

Note: Dictations may include ties, but will *not* include rests.

2.27

2.28

2.29

2.30

2.31

2.32

2.33

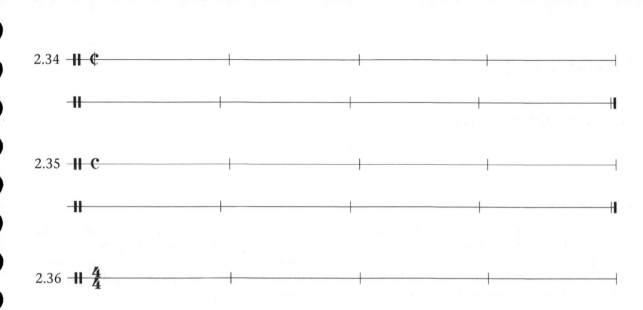

MODULE 3

Simple Meters, Triple

Introduction

Triple meters have three beats in a bar and are typically associated with dances, such as the waltz, the minuet, and the ländler. The typical emphasis pattern in a triple meter makes beat 1 the strongest beat and beat 2 the weakest. The emphasis on beat 3 is somewhere between beats 1 and 2 in strength and serves to make beat 3 lead into the subsequent downbeat. Work towards projecting this "strong–weak–upbeat" emphasis pattern within the meter at various tempos.

No new beat patterns will be introduced in this module.

Rhythms for Performance

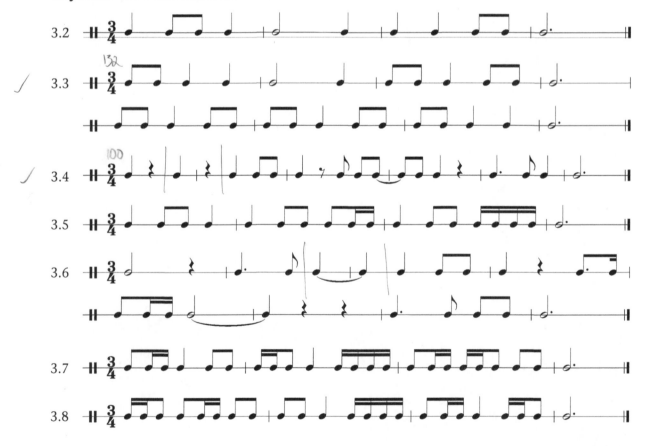

Dictation Practice

Note: Dictations may include ties, but will *not* include rests.

3.28 $\frac{3}{4}$

3.29 $\frac{3}{4}$

3.30 $\frac{3}{4}$

3.31 $\frac{3}{4}$

3.32 $\frac{3}{4}$

3.33 $\frac{3}{4}$

3.34 $\frac{3}{4}$

3.35 $\frac{3}{2}$

3.36 $\frac{3}{2}$

3.37 $\frac{3}{8}$

MODULE 4

Syncopation in Simple Meters

Introduction

Syncopated rhythms deliberately work against the natural emphasis of a meter by emphasizing the beats and portions of beats that are ordinarily unaccented. Such beats are commonly referred to as "weak." The most typical syncopation rhythm is the *short–long–short* pattern that is shown at three metric levels in Example 4.1. Under bracket 1, the syncopation figure emphasizes beats 2 and 4; under bracket 2, it emphasizes the second eighth-note in beats 3 and 4; and under bracket 3, it emphasizes the second and fourth sixteenth-notes of beat 2.

Ties can be used to displace the syncopation figure, as in Example 4.2.

Notice that the effect of the syncopation rhythm becomes more pronounced as the note values get shorter, which is why you have already encountered the rhythm under bracket 1 in earlier modules. Practice Examples 4.1 and 4.2 until you are familiar with these basic patterns.

Paradigms

The following beat patterns will be introduced in this module.

4.3

Rhythms for Performance

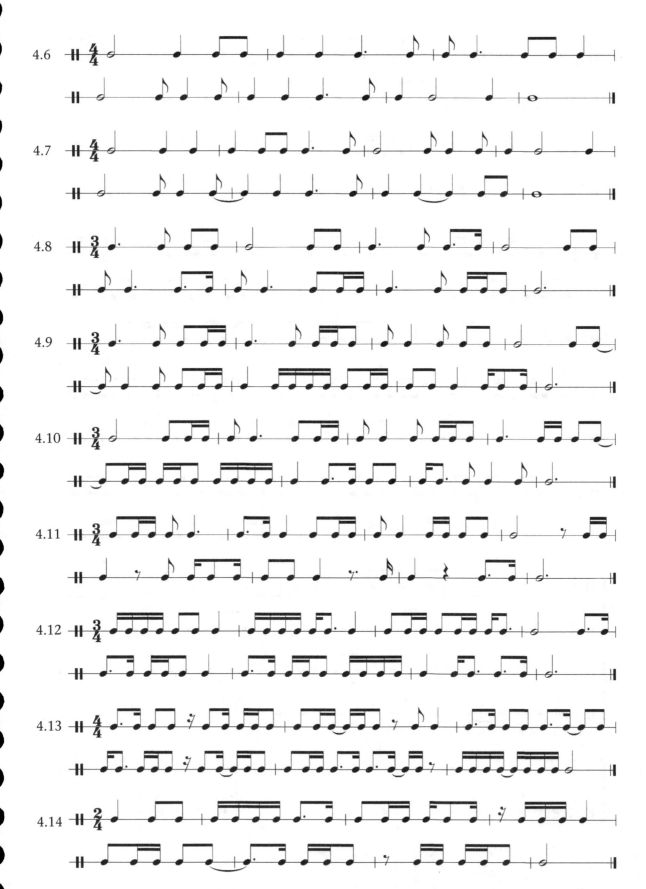

4.15

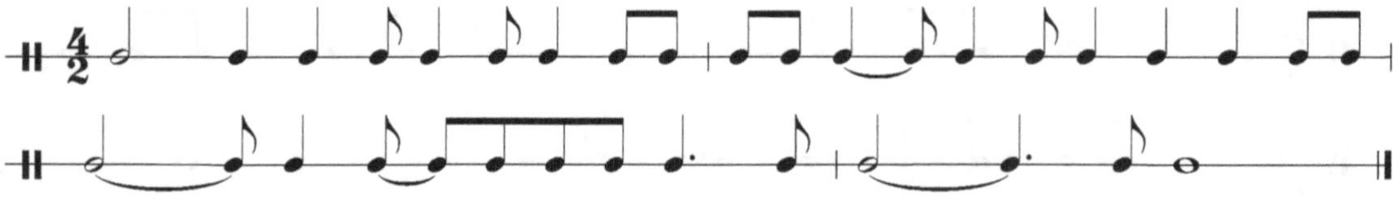

4.16

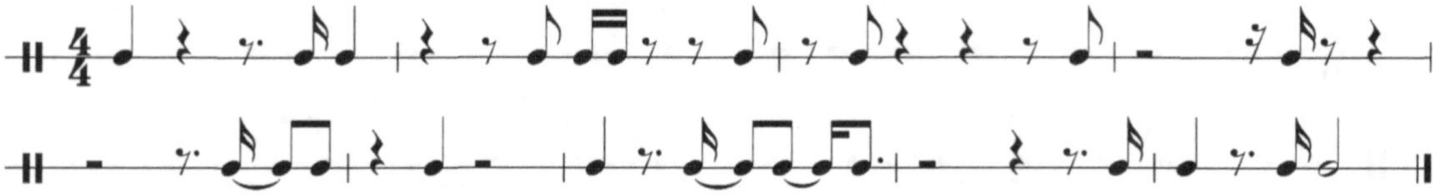

4.17

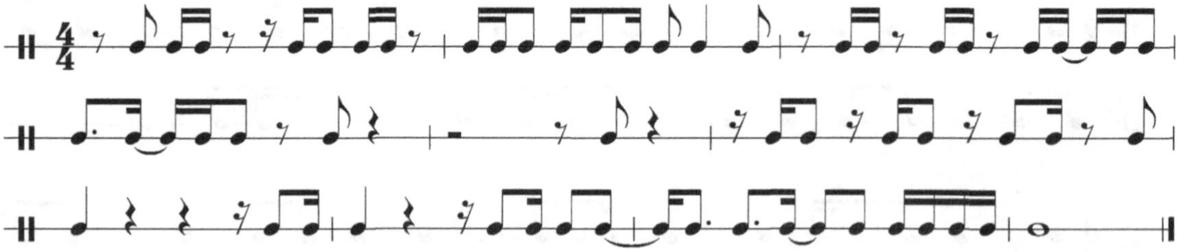

4.18

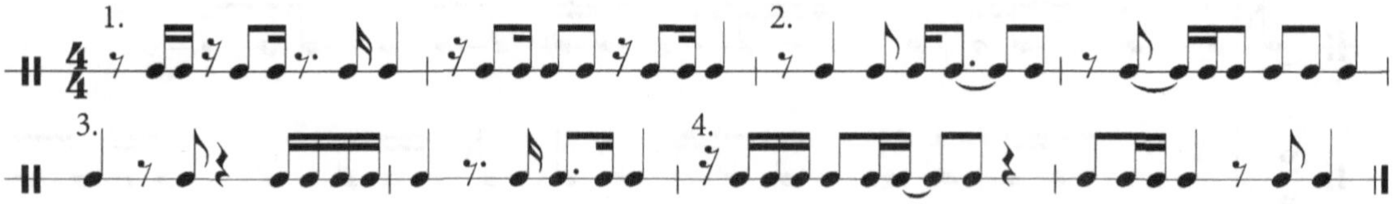

4.19

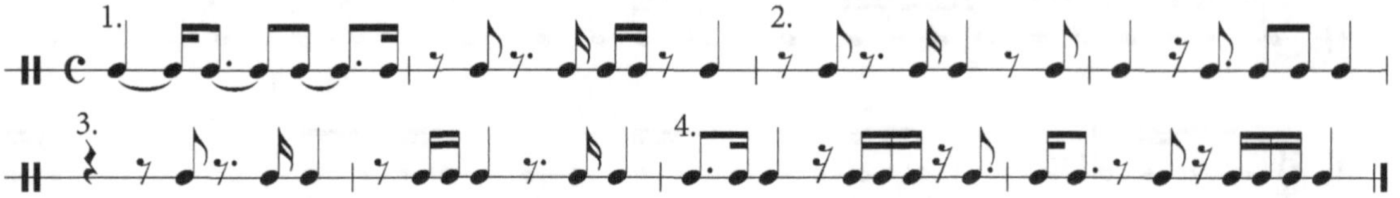

4.20

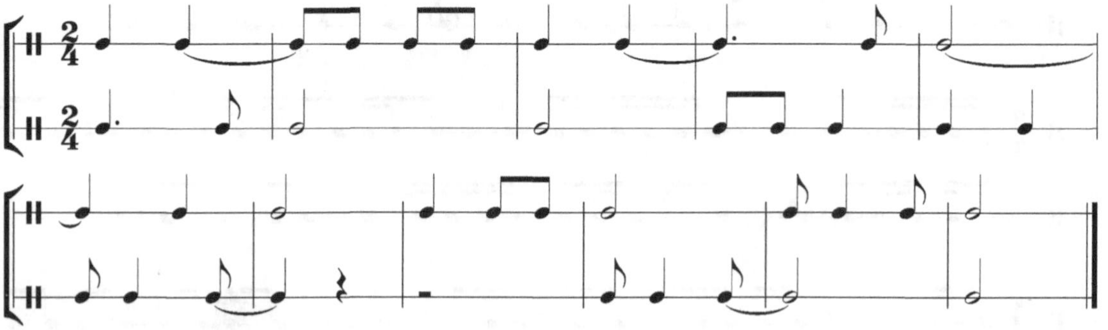

4.21

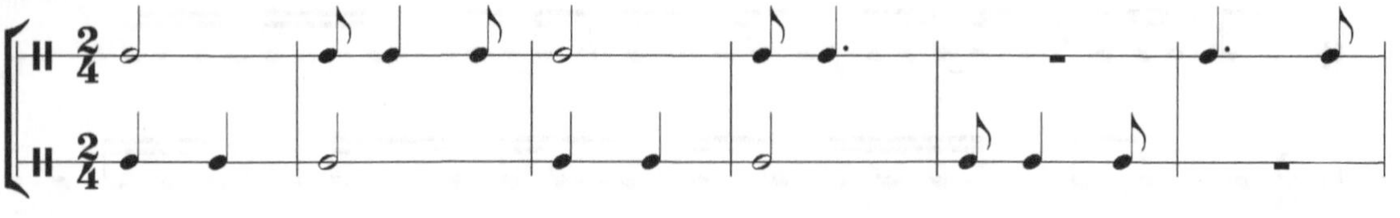

4.29

4.30

Dictation Practice

Note: Dictations may include ties, but will *not* include rests.

4.31

4.32

4.33

4.34

4.35

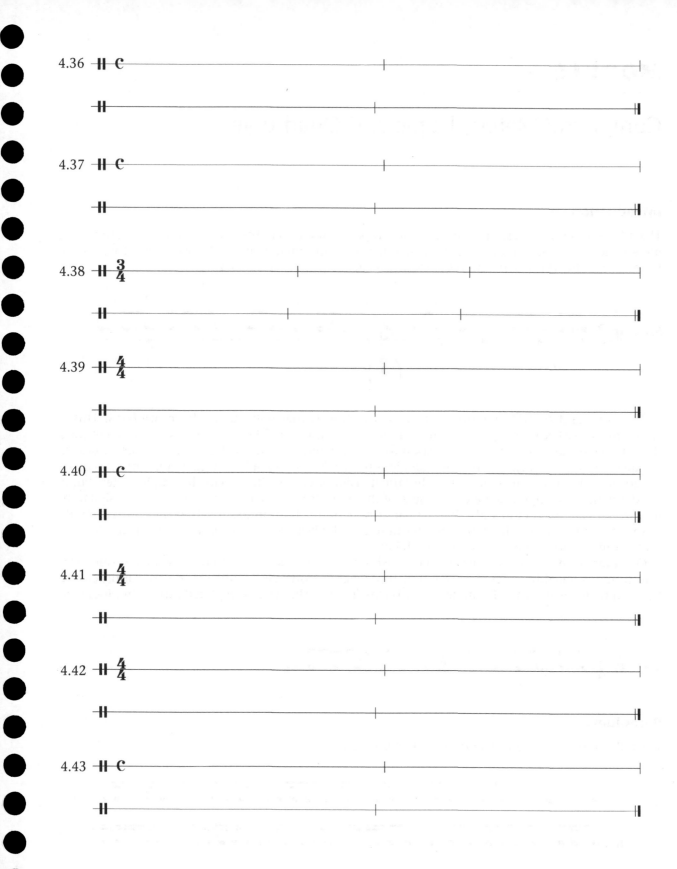

MODULE 5

Compound Meters, Duple and Quadruple

Introduction

The difference between a simple meter and a compound meter is in the division of the beat. In simple meters the beat divides into two parts while in compound meters the beat divides into three parts. Example 5.1 shows the correlation between two bars of $\frac{2}{4}$ and two bars of $\frac{6}{8}$.

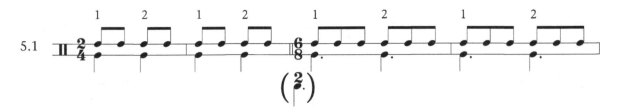

The important thing to recognize in this correlation is that both meters have *two beats*. This is counterintuitive because in $\frac{2}{4}$ the top number means that there are 2 beats in a measure, which implies that in $\frac{6}{8}$ there should be 6 beats. The reason for this difference lies in the fact that the note values we use divide into pairs (i.e., a whole-note divides into *two* half-notes, a half-note divides into *two* quarter-notes, and so on). This scheme matches the division into twos that occurs in simple meters but is at odds with the compound meter's division of the beat into three parts. An accurate meter signature for $\frac{6}{8}$ would have a 2 on top and a dotted quarter-note on the bottom to show that there are two beats in the measure and that the dotted quarter-note gets the beat. As you work through this module try to perform the *true* number of beats in each bar.

One more thing to note is the close relationship between $\frac{3}{4}$ and $\frac{6}{8}$. In both of these meters one measure contains 6 eighth-notes. The way that those eighth-notes are grouped is the crucial difference between them, as shown in Example 5.2. This close relationship will be explored further in Module 8.

Paradigms

The following beat patterns will be used in this module.

Rhythms for Performance

In the next three examples all the note values are doubled, relative to $\frac{6}{8}$. What note value gets the beat now?

5.28

Dictation Practice

Note: Dictations may include ties, but will *not* include rests.

5.29 $\frac{6}{8}$

5.30 $\frac{6}{8}$

5.31 $\frac{6}{8}$

5.32 $\frac{6}{8}$

5.33 $\frac{6}{8}$

5.34 $\frac{6}{8}$

5.35 $\frac{6}{8}$

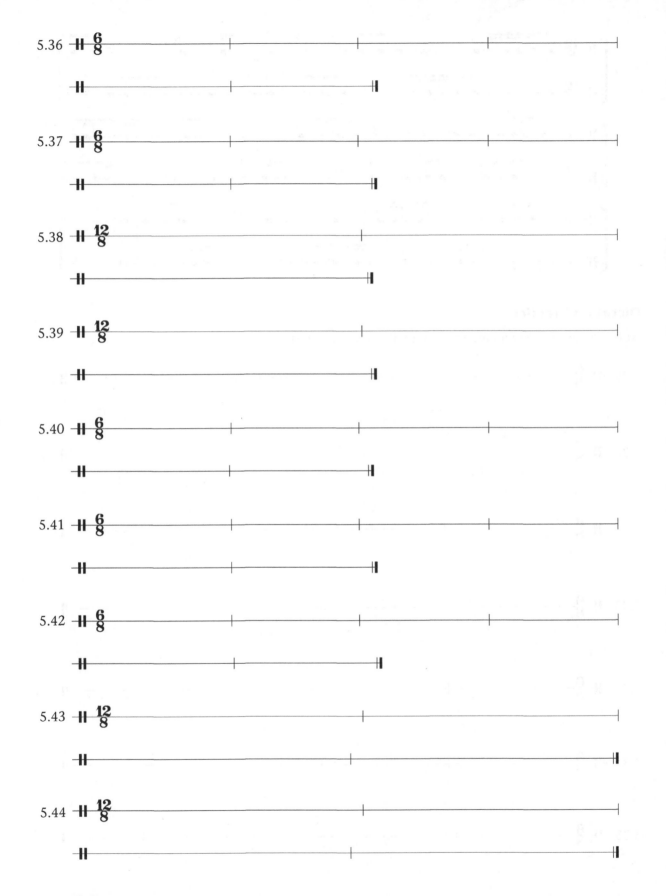

MODULE 6

Compound Meters, Triple

Introduction

This module combines two skills you have already studied: triple meters and compound division of the beat. Because works are set in a triple compound meter so infrequently it will feel foreign to you at first, but work sincerely and carefully until you are fluent in this meter.

Paradigms

No new beat patterns appear in this module.

Rhythms for Performance

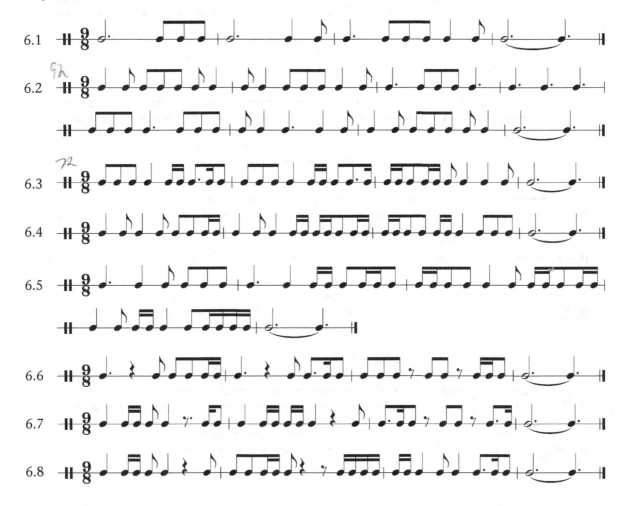

6.9

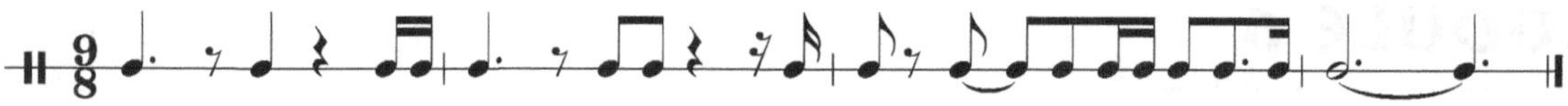

6.10

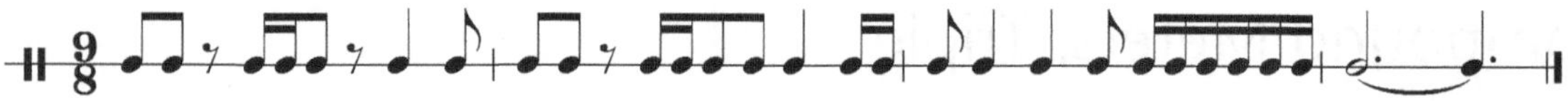

6.11

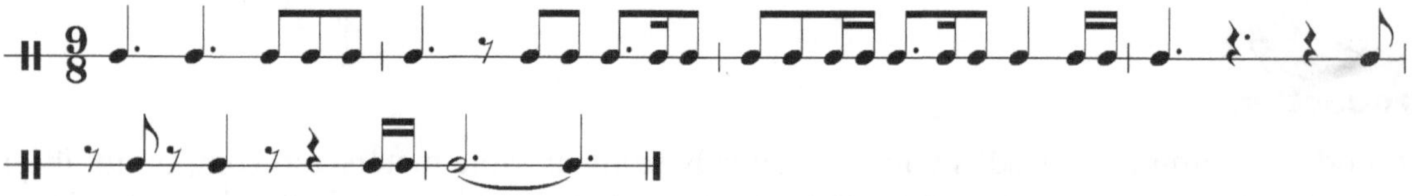

6.12

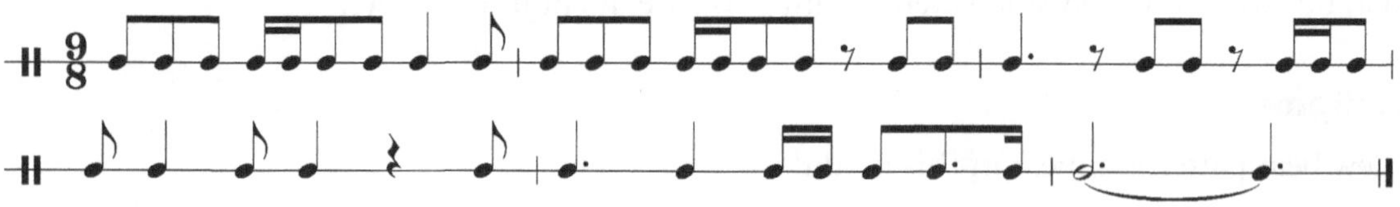

6.13

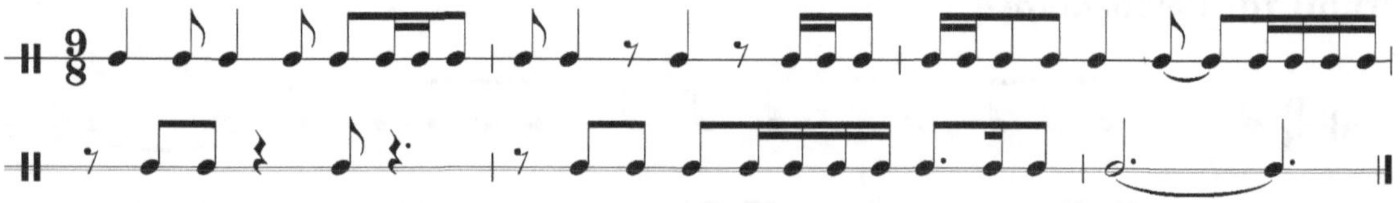

6.14

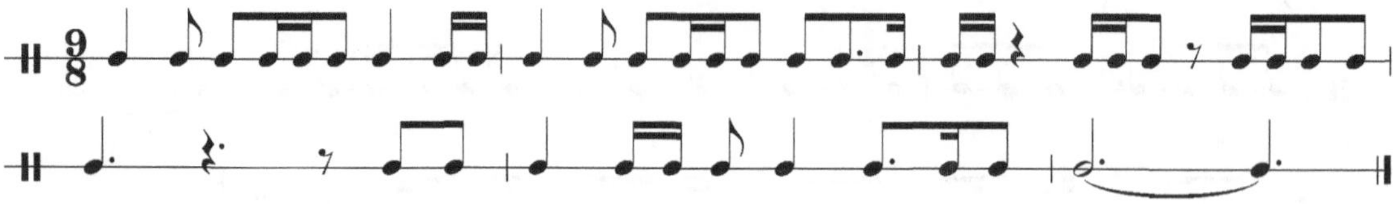

6.15

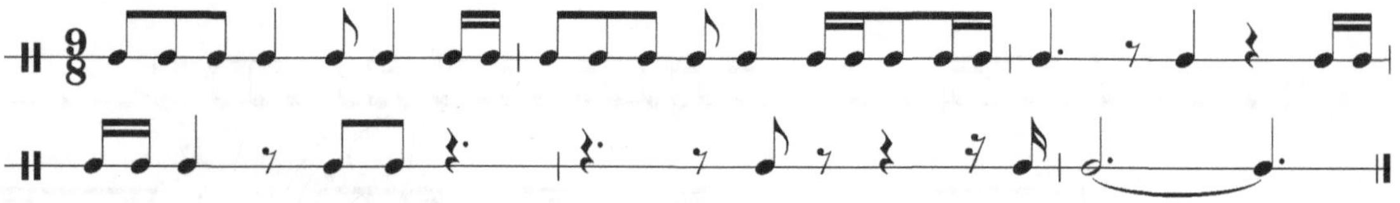

6.16

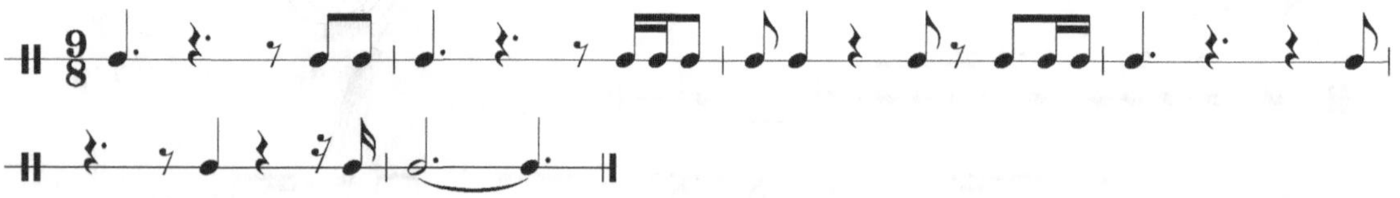

6.17

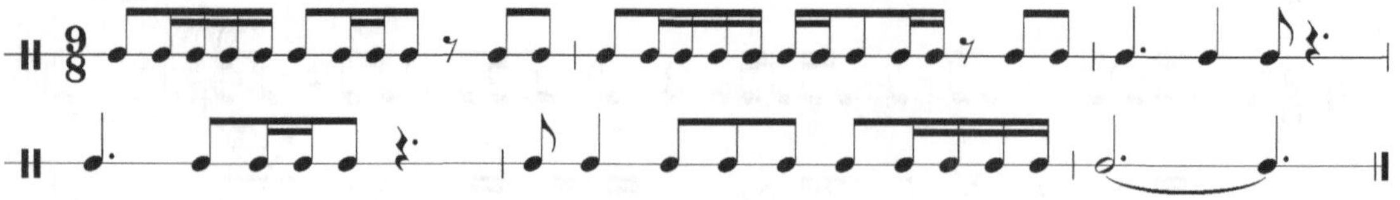

6.18
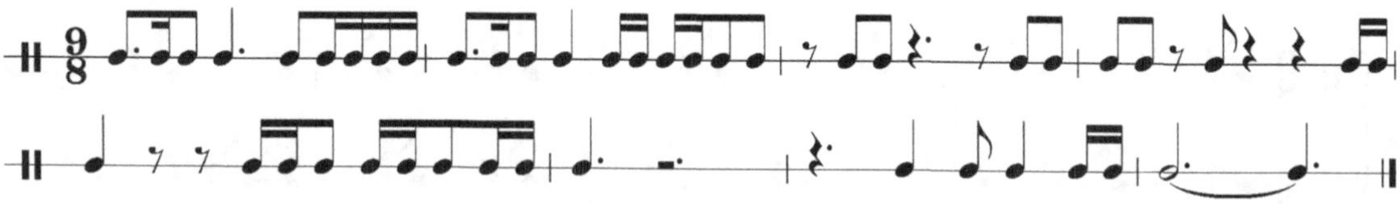

6.19
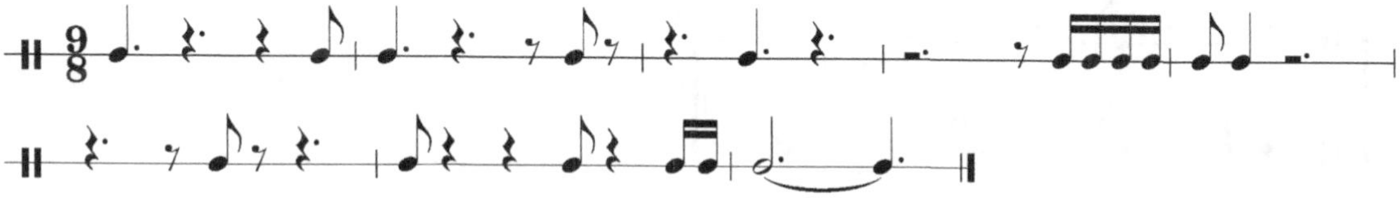

6.20
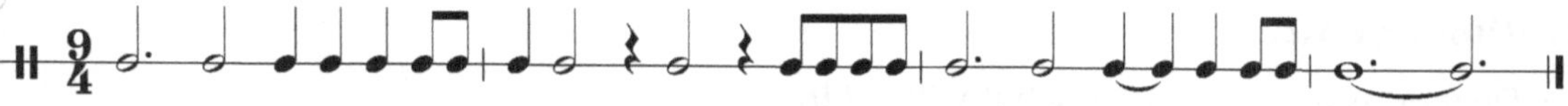

6.21
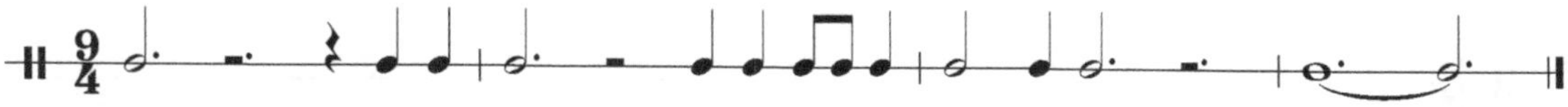

6.22
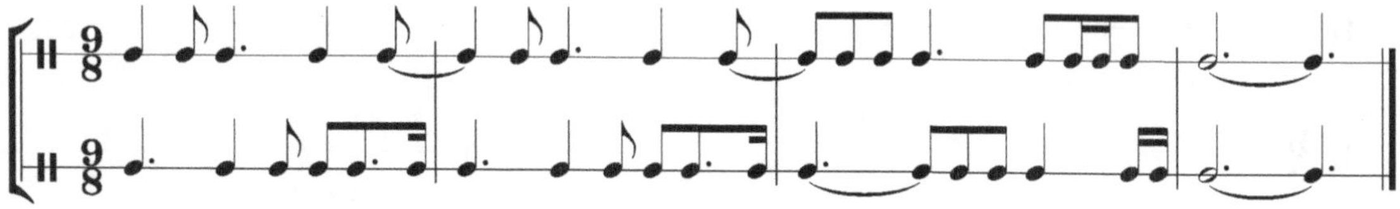

6.23
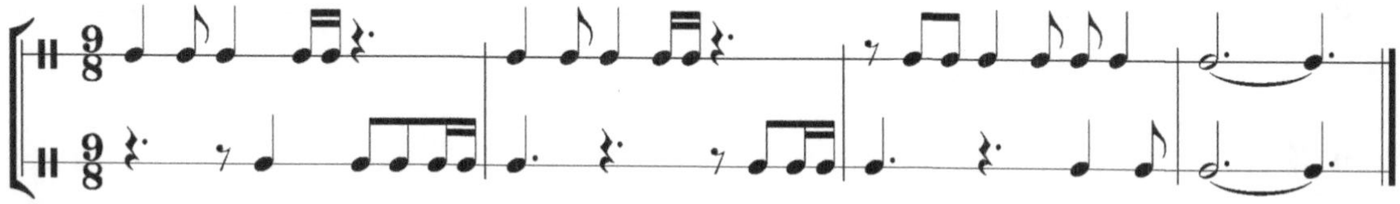

6.24
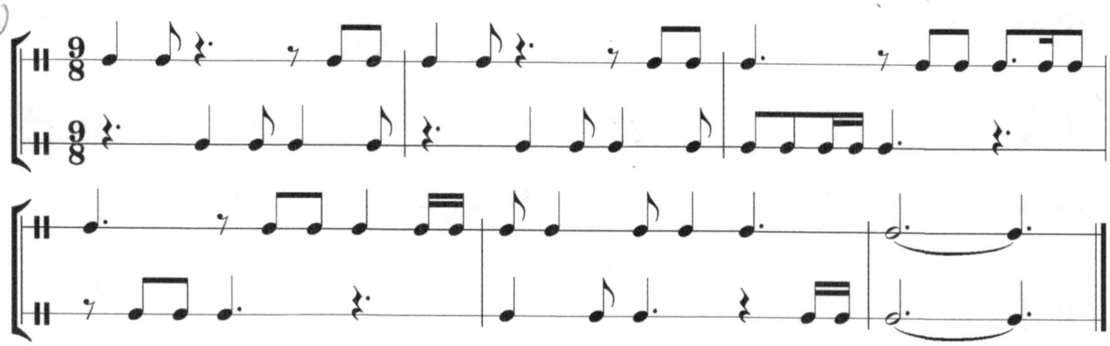

6.25
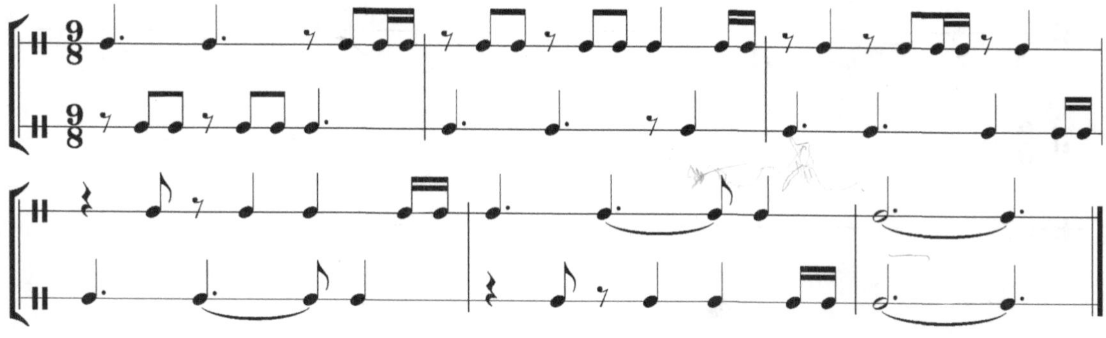

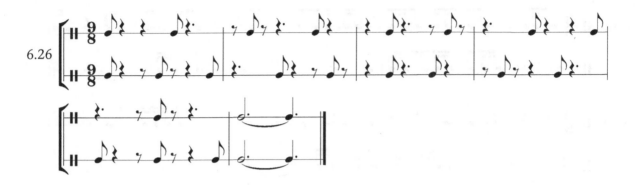

6.26

Dictation Practice

Note: Dictations may include ties, but will *not* include rests.

6.27

6.28

6.29

6.30

6.31

6.32

6.33 $\|\frac{9}{8}$

6.34 $\|\frac{9}{8}$

6.35 $\|\frac{9}{8}$

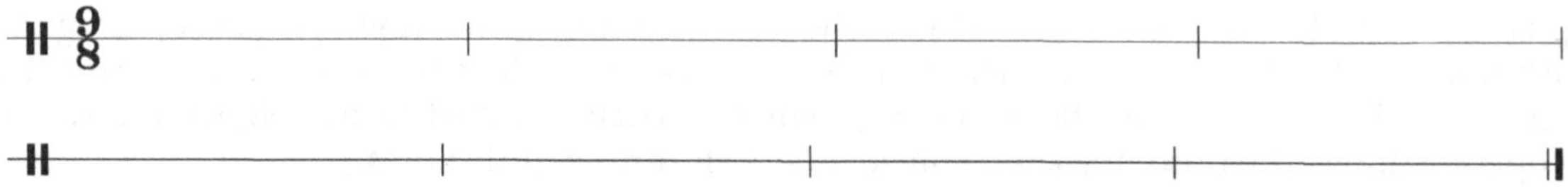

6.36 $\|\frac{9}{8}$

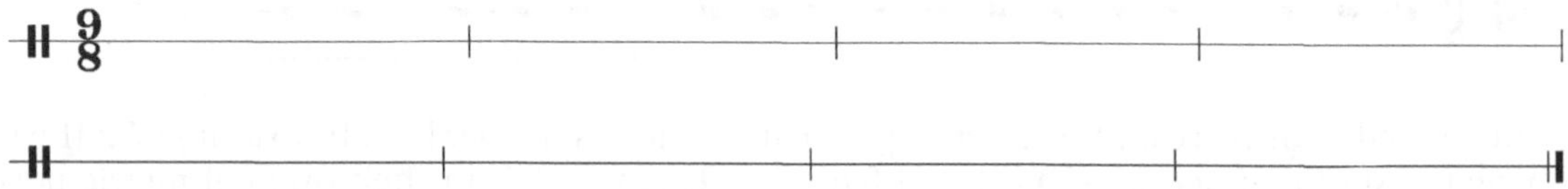

MODULE 7

Syncopation in Compound Meters

Introduction

As with simple meters, syncopations in compound meters temporarily destabilize the natural pattern of emphasis. Consider Example 7.1, which shows three different ways of syncopating at the eighth-note level within one beat. The syncopation above the first bracket occurs in the last two eighth-notes. The syncopation above the second bracket occurs in the first two eighth-notes. And the syncopation above the third bracket is spread across all three eighth-notes.

7.1

Ties can be used to displace and/or extend syncopations across the bar line. In Example 7.2 the brackets above the staff correspond to bracketed figures in Example 7.1, in their original metric position. The brackets below the staff show how you can also relate these figures to the third syncopation in 7.1, but starting on the second or third eighth-notes of the beat.

7.2

Paradigms

The following beat patterns will be added in this module.

7.3

Rhythms for Performance

7.4

7.5

7.6

Dictation Practice

Note: Dictations may include ties, but will *not* include rests.

7.23

7.24

7.25

7.26

7.27

7.28 $\frac{6}{8}$

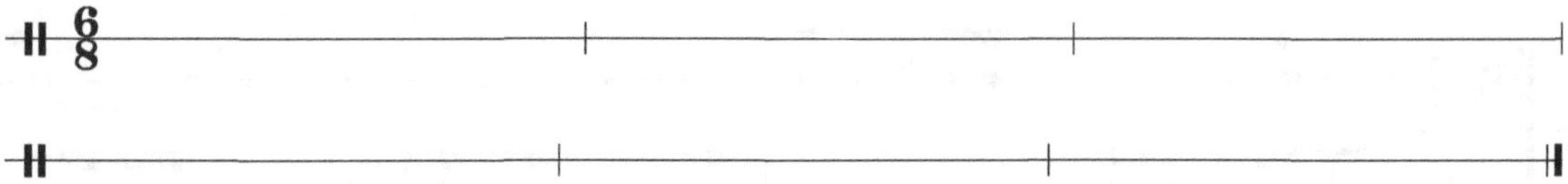

7.29 $\frac{6}{8}$

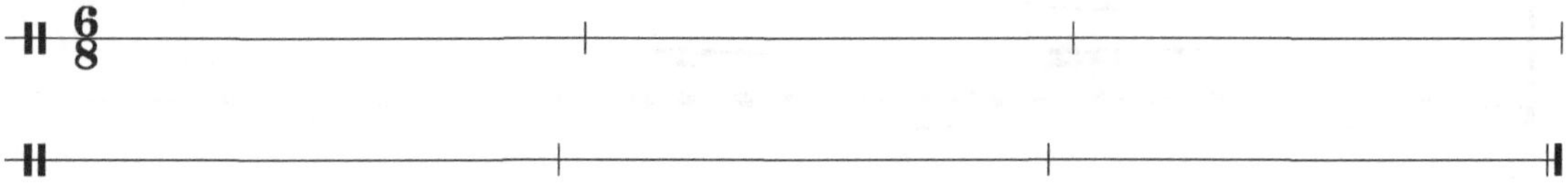

7.30 $\frac{6}{8}$

7.31 $\frac{6}{8}$

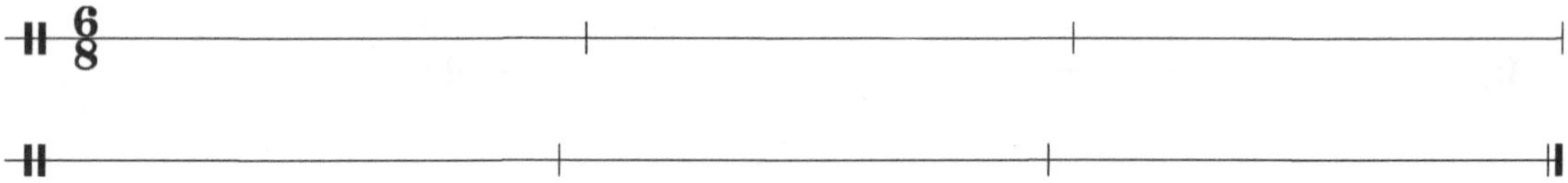

7.32 $\frac{6}{8}$

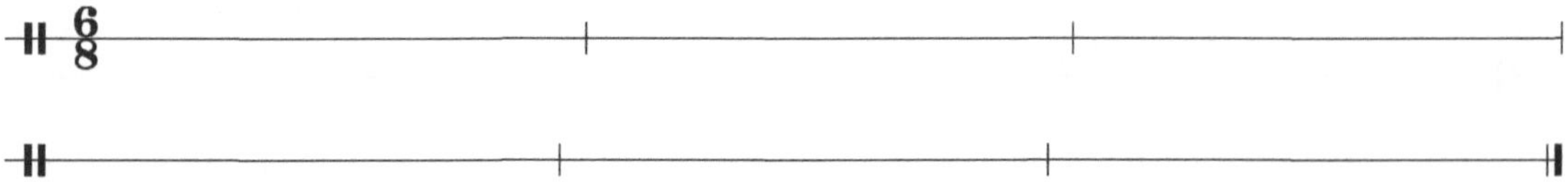

MODULE 8

Triplets, Duplets, and Hemiola

Introduction

Triplets and duplets can be thought of as a temporary shift between duple and compound meters, as if a beat or two has been borrowed from one subdivision to the other. Of the two borrowings, the triplet is the more common one by far. Example 8.1a is in $\frac{6}{8}$ and 8.1b is in $\frac{2}{4}$, but they will sound *identical* in performance. Although it is relatively rare, it is also possible to borrow a duple subdivision from simple meters while in a compound meter; Example 8.1c sounds exactly like Example 8.1d.

Notice how triplets and duplets are notated, with a 3 or a 2 (and sometimes a bracket, as seen in Example 8.2) calling your attention to them and allowing you to anticipate their performance while sight reading.

Paradigms

The following beats can appear in simple meters (with the quarter-note being the beat).

8.2

The following beats can appear in compound meters (with the dotted quarter-note being the beat). The first beat pattern is technically new, although it sounds exactly like the duplet in the second measure.

8.3

Quarter-note triplets are slightly different, but only because they span two beats. As with most counting challenges, the solution is to subdivide. In Example 8.4, measures a and b sound identical.

8.4

Hemiola refers to a special form of interplay that is possible between simple-triple and duple-compound meters. Think of $\frac{3}{4}$ and $\frac{6}{8}$, both of which have six eighth-notes in a measure, which allows composers to blend them rather easily and without any special notation. The effect of hemiola is similar to that of a triplet or a duplet in that it seems as though the notated meter is temporarily suspended, although the shifts are somewhat less temporary in the case of hemiola. Consider Example 8.5, in which a line in $\frac{3}{4}$ is notated over a line in $\frac{6}{8}$. Bars 1 and 2 conform to the standard beats in each meter. In measure 2, however, a tie is used in the $\frac{6}{8}$ line to make it match the beats in $\frac{3}{4}$, while ties are used in m. 4 to make the $\frac{3}{4}$ line sound like a measure in $\frac{6}{8}$.

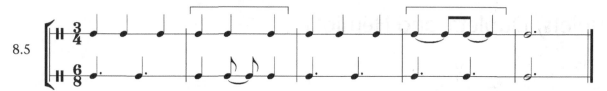

Another form of hemiola can occur between $\frac{3}{4}$ and $\frac{3}{2}$, as shown in Example 8.6. Measures 1–2 and mm. 7–8 are clearly in $\frac{3}{4}$, while mm. 3–4 can be performed as a single measure in $\frac{3}{2}$, as can mm. 5–6. Because it can be difficult to recognize this kind of hemiola, accents will be used in this module to draw your attention to measures that should be performed as such.

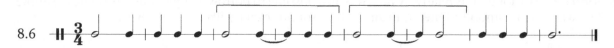

Even at the eighth-note level, recognizing a hemiola on the page can be tricky, so pay special attention to the beaming of eighth-notes and the use of "misplaced" quarter-notes, both of which will alert you to perform a hemiola.

Rhythms for Performance

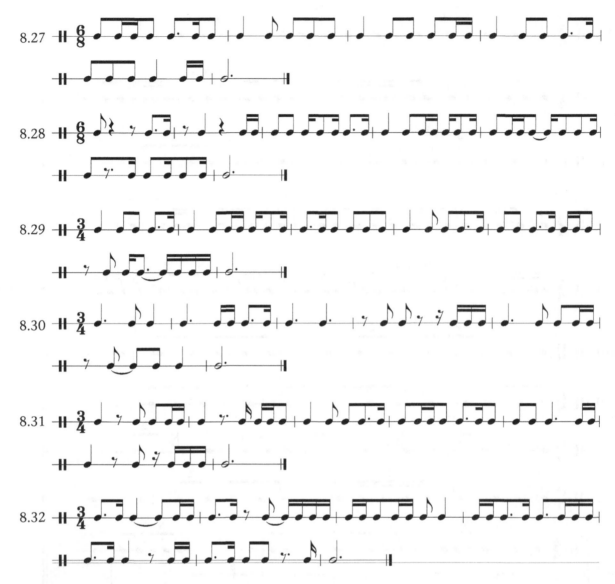

To experience the hemiola, the next four examples should be performed at a quick tempo.

8.35

Allegro assai (♩=160)

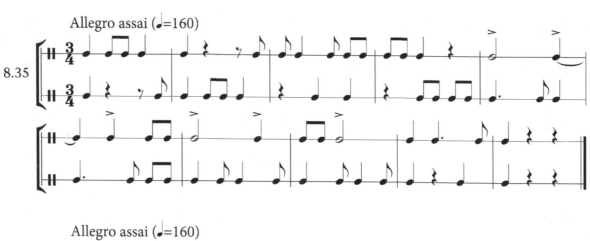

8.36

Allegro assai (♩=160)

8.37

Dictation Practice

8.38 $\frac{4}{4}$

8.39 $\frac{2}{4}$

8.40 $\frac{4}{4}$

8.41 $\frac{4}{4}$

8.42 $\frac{2}{4}$

8.43 $\frac{4}{4}$

8.44 $\frac{6}{8}$

8.45 $\frac{6}{8}$

8.46 $\frac{6}{8}$

8.47 $\frac{3}{4}$

8.48 $\frac{3}{4}$

8.49 $\frac{3}{4}$

8.50 $\frac{6}{8}$

8.51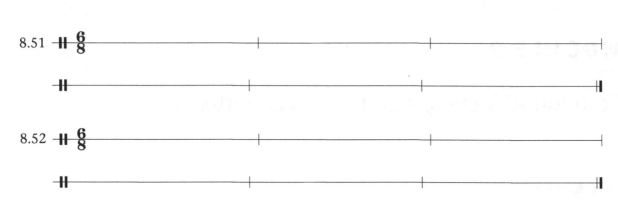

8.52

8.53

MODULE 9

Compound Meters, Advanced Beat Patterns

Introduction

In this module you will continue to practice working in compound meters and four new beat patterns will be added to the growing list of possibilities.

Paradigms

The following beat patterns will be used in this module.

Rhythms for Performance

9.10
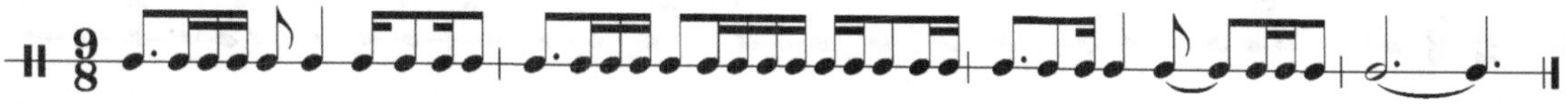

9.11
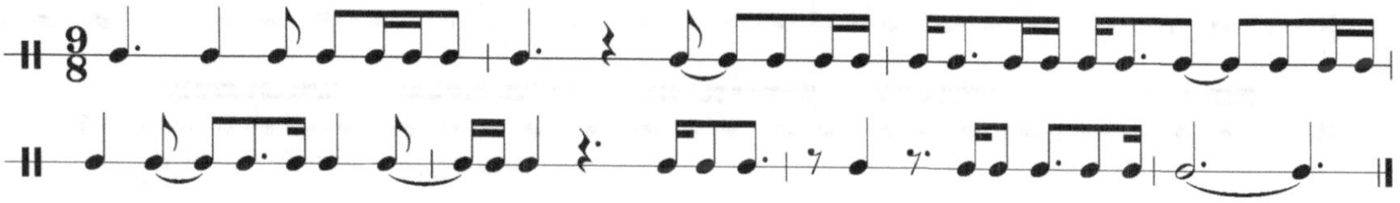

9.12
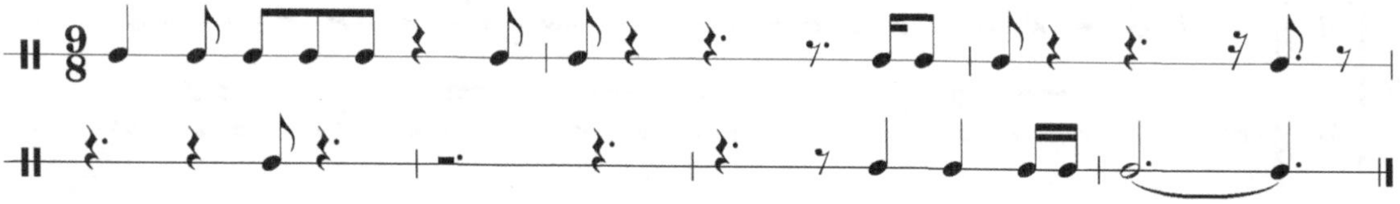

9.13
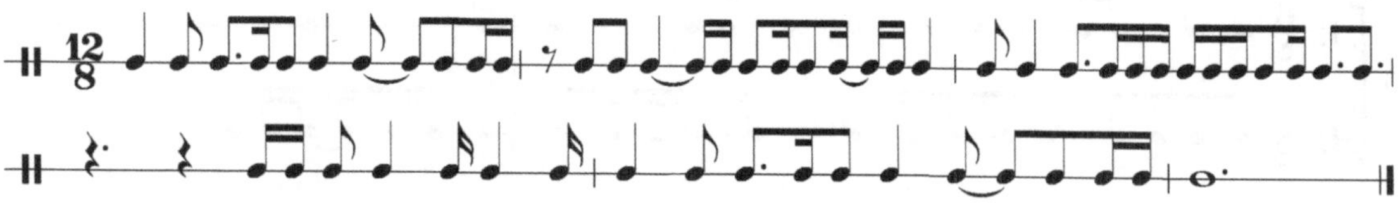

9.14
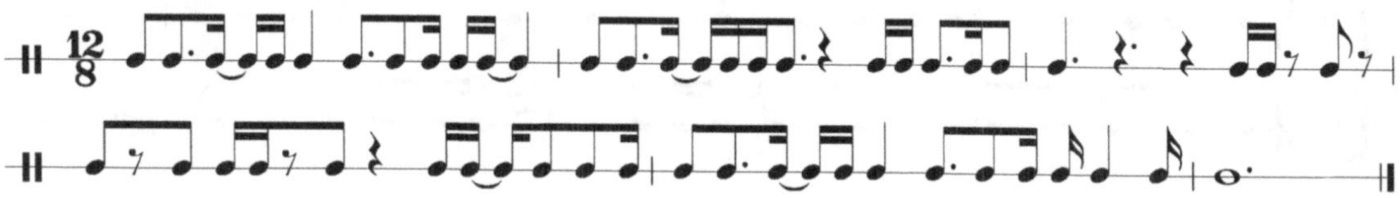

9.15
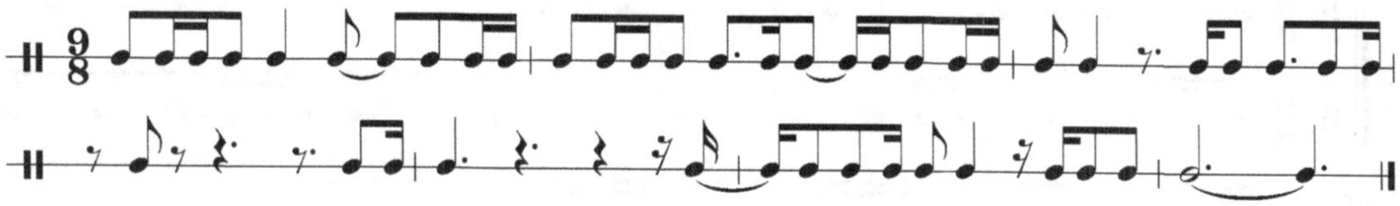

9.16
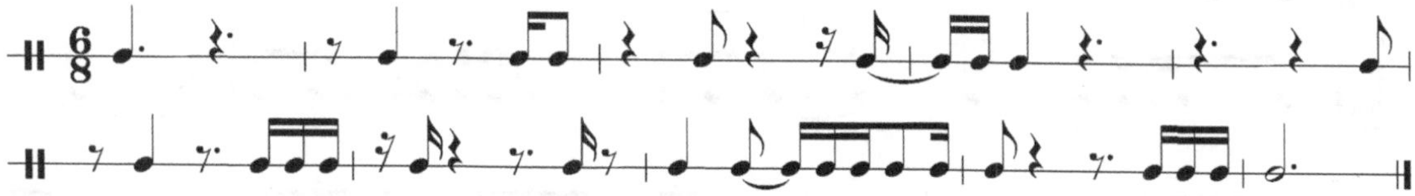

9.17
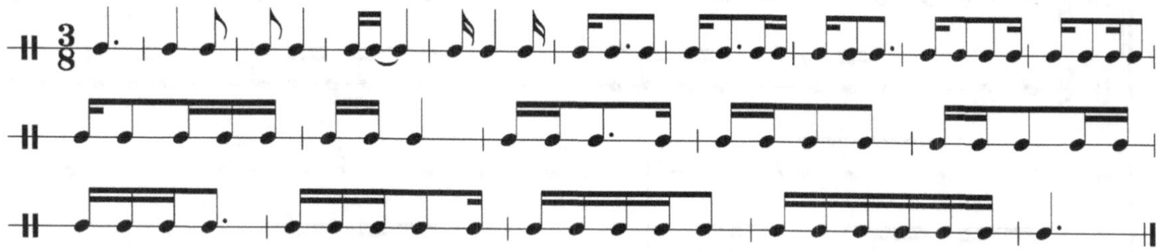

9.24

Dictation Practice

Note: Dictations may include ties, but will *not* include rests.

9.25

9.26

9.27

9.28

9.29

9.30

9.31 $\frac{6}{8}$

9.32 $\frac{9}{8}$

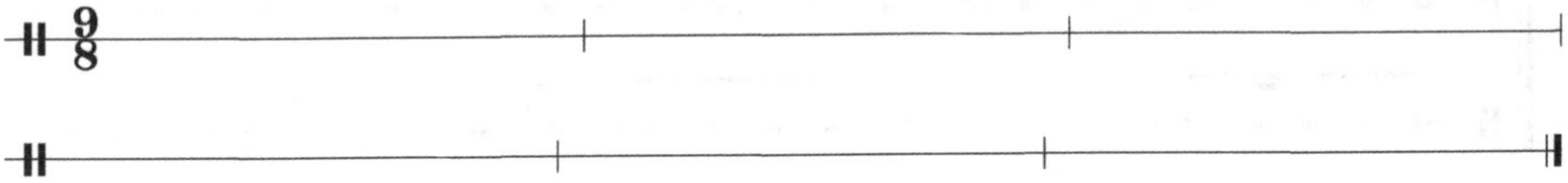

9.33 $\frac{9}{8}$

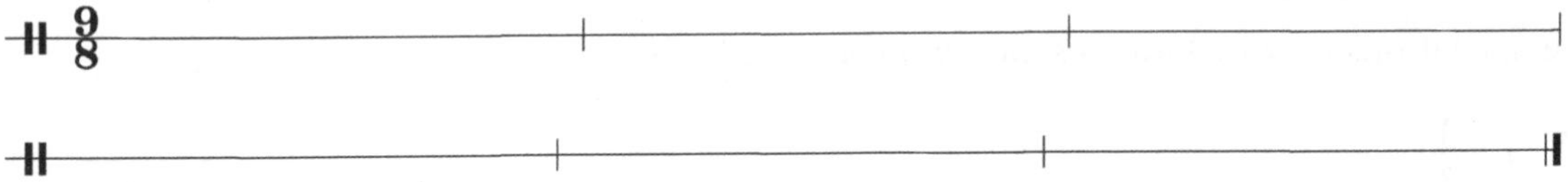

9.34 $\frac{12}{8}$

MODULE 10

Asymmetrical and Mixed Meters

Introduction

This module is dedicated to rhythmic possibilities that are most often found in post-tonal and world music. Asymmetrical meters are those that don't divide into equal portions on at least one level. Example 10.1 shows that $\frac{5}{4}$ has two strong beats and that they are spaced unequally, dividing the bar into either 2 beats + 3 beats, or 3 beats + 2 beats.

Example 10.2 shows asymmetry at the level of the subdivision of the beat. It is possible to think of $\frac{5}{8}$ as a hybridization of $\frac{2}{4}$ and $\frac{6}{8}$, since each bar in $\frac{5}{8}$ has one beat that divides into two eighth-notes and another beat that divides into three. In practice, composers can choose to write music that is consistently set in 2+3 or in 3+2, or that goes back and forth between the two. Notice that the beaming of eighth-notes will let you know whether you are to perform it as 2+3 or as 3+2.

Example 10.3 shows three different configurations for $\frac{7}{8}$ time. Just as we thought of $\frac{5}{8}$ as a simple/compound hybrid, it is also possible to think of $\frac{7}{8}$ as a triple meter that has two simple beats and one compound beat. Again, take note of the beaming, which groups eighth-notes into easily recognized beats.

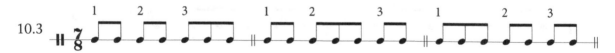

The meters shown in Example 10.4 are something like $\frac{7}{8}$ in that both have three beats per measure such that two beats are the same and one beat is different. The difference is that the meters in 10.4 have two compound beats and just one simple beat.

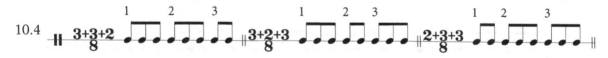

The last new meter that will be introduced in this module is $\frac{7}{4}$. This meter is somewhat nebulous and lacks clear analogies with previously encountered meters. Just keep the beat steady and try to emphasize downbeats, as in any other meter.

In addition to these new meters, this module also contains several examples of what is known as mixed or changing meters. In these examples the prevailing meter will occasionally shift from one number of beats in a measure to another. For the purposes of this module the beat will always be represented by the quarter-note, which makes these metric shifts easier to perform. Be aware, though, that composers are under no such constraints and you are likely to encounter various types of shifts in freely composed music.

Rhythms for Performance

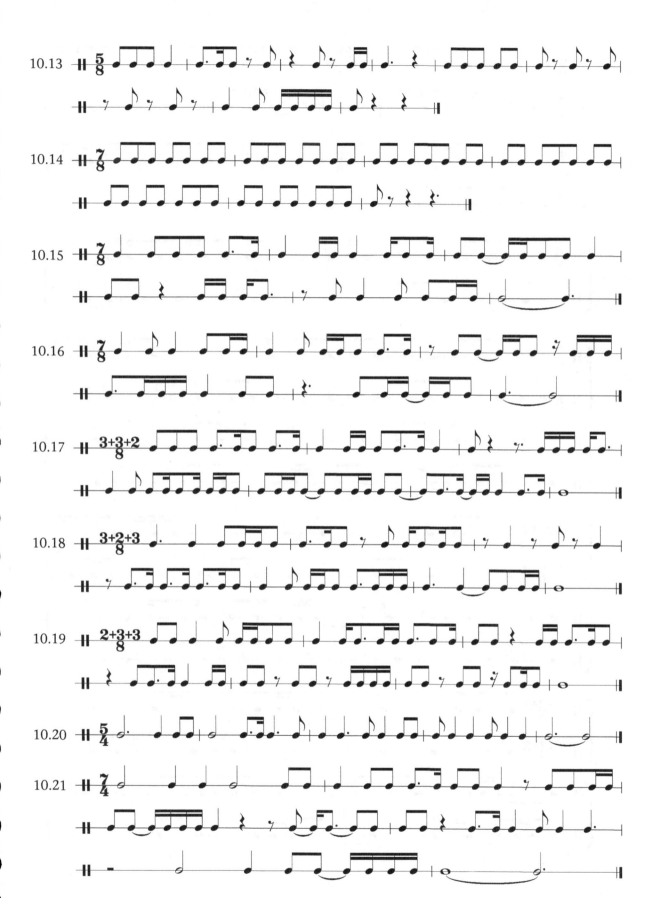

Dictation Practice

Note: Dictations may include ties, but will *not* include rests.

10.28 $\frac{5}{8}$

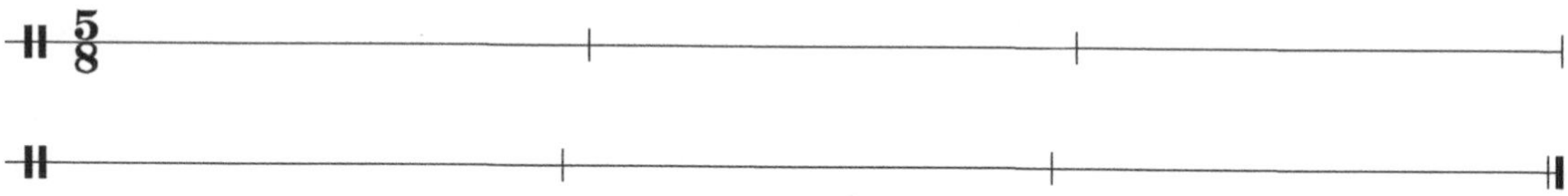

10.29 $\frac{7}{8}$

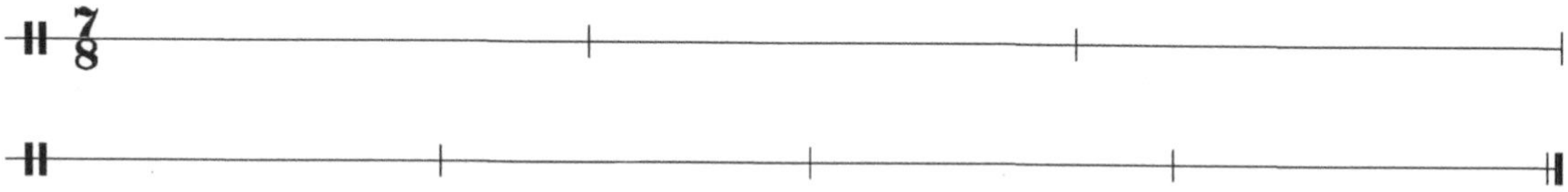

10.30 $\frac{3+3+2}{8}$

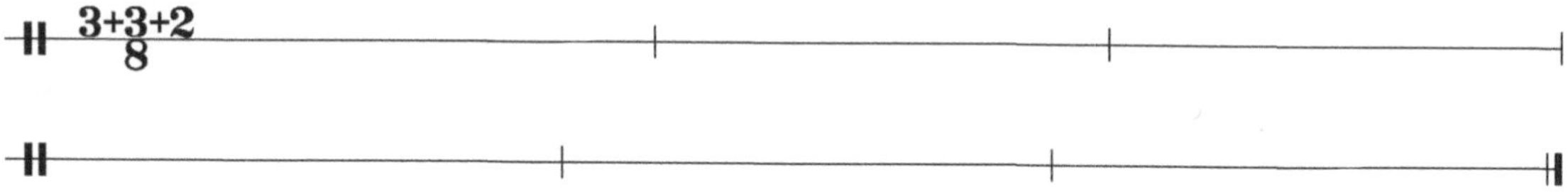

10.31 $\frac{3+2+3}{8}$

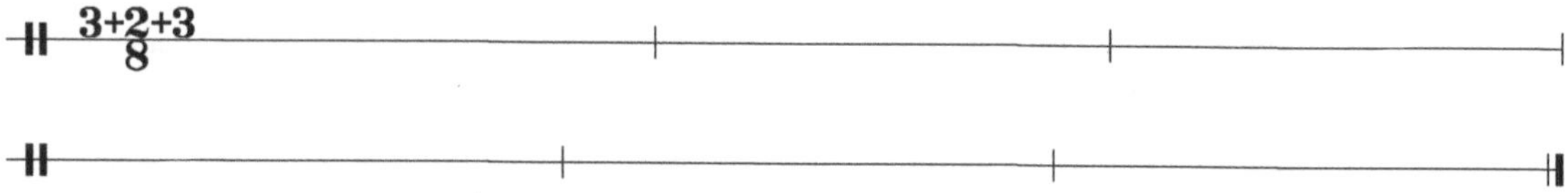

10.32 $\frac{4}{4}$ $\frac{3}{4}$ $\frac{2}{4}$ $\frac{5}{4}$ $\frac{4}{4}$

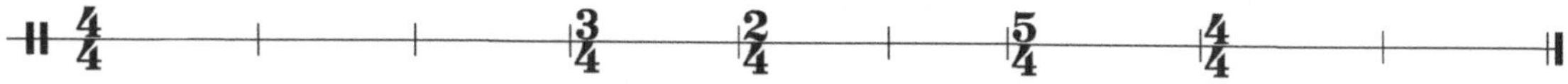

PART 2

Melody

MODULE 1

Steps within the Major Scale

The Dictation Keys for Part 2 can be found at the end of the book (pages 294–326)

Clefs

Although this book assumes at least a passing familiarity with the basics of musical notation, it is nevertheless wise to begin with a bit of information on how to "decode" a melody. Example 1.1 shows the same note, middle C, in four different clefs. Reading from left to right, they are the Bass, Tenor, Alto, and Treble clefs. There are four different clefs because voices and many instruments perform in a relatively limited range. So, rather than use an excessive number of *ledger lines* (temporary extensions beyond the five permanent lines of the staff) to extend the staff, which can make notes difficult to read, we change what the lines and spaces mean via a clef. This way we can accommodate the *range* of a voice or instrument with relative ease. Notice that the Tenor and Alto clefs are actually the same clef on different lines, and that middle C is always the line that goes through the middle of the clef. In both the Bass and Treble clefs middle C sits on a ledger line above or below the staff.

1.1

As an illustration of notes that fit comfortably within a clef and those that require an excessive number of ledger lines, Example 1.2a shows the exact same melodic motive in all four clefs. Example 1.2b shows the same melody notated an octave higher, again, in all four clefs.

1.2

When the melody in Example 1.2a is notated in the Bass and Tenor clefs it fits comfortably within the staff. When notated in the Treble clef, however, an unwieldy number of ledger lines is required, making the melody rather difficult to read. When the same melody is notated an octave higher, the Alto and Treble clefs become more reasonable choices.

Scales

Example 1.3a shows a C-major scale that ascends from middle C to the C an octave above it. The individual notes that make up a scale are known as *scale degrees*. Each scale degree has a name, and as you get to know the scale better you may come to recognize each scale degree as something like a character in a story, with its own set of qualities, associations, and motivations. In fact, your teacher may ask you to use a unique number or solfège syllable as you sing each scale degree, which is something like calling its name every time you sing it. Practice singing this scale in a comfortable octave and at a comfortable tempo. Pay attention to your intonation and practice both ascending and descending versions.

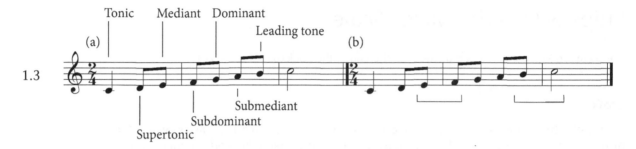

The brackets under Example 1.3b indicate two special intervals known as half-steps, which in a major scale are always between scale degrees $\hat{3}$ and $\hat{4}$ and between scale degrees $\hat{7}$ and $\hat{1}$. Because all the other intervals in the scale are whole-steps, these half-steps give the major scale its characteristic sound. Notice that $\hat{7}$ is called the leading-tone and that it is a member of one of those half-steps. Its name refers to the fact that $\hat{7}$ is usually heard as unstable and wanting to lead upward (or resolve to) the far more stable tonic. The next scale degree that can be heard as unstable is the subdominant, which is the upper member of the other half-step and often causes us to anticipate a downward resolution, to the more stable mediant.

Scale degrees $\hat{4}$ and $\hat{7}$ are known as *tendency tones* and are crucial to a proper understanding of the major scale; you should get to know them well. Listen for them in the music you hear on the radio, in your rehearsals, and in movie soundtracks, and you will soon learn to recognize them and the sense of tension and resolution they can give to music.

In Example 1.4 a C major scale is shown side by side with a G major scale. Although these two scales begin and end on different notes, they will sound rather alike because of the *key signature*, the sharp just under the "(b)" that replaces F with F♯, thereby moving one of the half-steps from between E and F to between F♯ and G. When the key changes, so do the scale degrees. In other words, C is no longer the tonic—G is the tonic. What scale degree is C in G major? What notes are the tendency tones in G major?

Example 1.5, which is in the key of F major, uses all the same scale degrees as Example 1.4, but in a different key. Also, instead of ascending through a complete octave it begins to descend after reaching the dominant scale degree.

Sight-singing

As you work your way through the melodies in this module (and the rest of this book), remember that your goal is to become proficient at singing a melody at sight and without the aid of an instrument. Because there are myriad details that go into even the simplest musical notation, it is a good idea to have a routine, a mental checklist that you go through as you approach any melody for the first time.

One suggestion is a simple left-to-right routine in which you take stock of the clef, the key signature, the meter, and the tonic, and *always in that order* so that you don't forget one. After that, it's a good idea to examine the range of the melody. Does it lie above, below, or on both sides of the tonic? These factors are probably sufficient for a first run-through, but you will also need to pay attention to tempo, dynamics, and phrasing in order to complete your interpretation of a melody.

Melodies for Performance

The swan sings teer-i-li-o, teer-i-li-o, teer-i-li-o.

Dictation Practice

1.31 **Andantino**

1.32 **Sustained**

1.33 **Sprightly**

1.34 **Senza fretta**

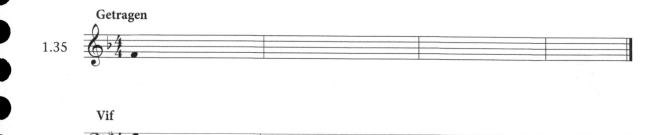

1.35 **Getragen**

1.36 **Vif**

1.37 **Gracieux**

1.38 **Animated**

1.39 **Sostenuto ed espressivo**

1.40 **Andantino**

MODULE 2

Steps within the Minor Scale

The minor scale differs from the major scale in three scale degrees: $\hat{3}$, $\hat{6}$, and $\hat{7}$, all of which are lowered by one half-step relative to their major-scale counterparts. Example 2.1 shows a C major scale next to a C-minor scale, with the flats making these differences obvious.

2.1

There are three types of minor scale (natural, harmonic, and melodic, Example 2.2) and you should learn how to sing each one correctly. The focus in these different versions of minor is clearly on the 6th and 7th scale degrees. The natural minor scale requires no accidentals, obeying the key signature precisely. The diatonic $\hat{7}$ that lies a whole-step from the tonic (known in this form as the subtonic) has traditionally been raised by a half-step in order to replicate the leading-tone as it occurs in the major scale; the result can be seen in the harmonic minor scale. The interval of an augmented second between $\hat{6}$ and $\hat{7}$ in harmonic minor can be awkward to sing. For this reason the melodic minor scale has ascending and descending versions of $\hat{6}$ and $\hat{7}$, allowing a minor-mode melody to have both a raised leading-tone and a lowered submediant, the latter of which maintains the characteristic sound of the minor mode.

2.2

The distinctions between these three forms of minor are commonly held in theory, but in practice it is common for music to exhibit all three interchangeably. This fluidity in pitch structure and the fact that we encounter minor less often than major mean that it takes more effort to become proficient in the minor mode.

One final consideration in minor is the nature of $\hat{6}$. Because it is lowered in minor, $\hat{6}$ lies a half-step above the far more stable $\hat{5}$ and is therefore a tendency tone. You might think that because lowered $\hat{3}$ is a half-step above the less stable $\hat{2}$, the latter would also be a tendency tone in minor. However, this is not the case. $\hat{4}$ remains a tendency tone in minor, even though its resolution to $\hat{3}$ is by a whole step. The last tendency tone in minor is $\hat{7}$ when it is raised to become the leading-tone, as in harmonic minor and in ascending melodic minor.

Melodies for Performance

2.24

Dictation Practice

Andante

2.25

Moderato

2.26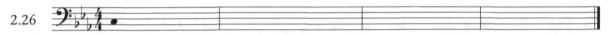

Triste

2.27

Con vivo

2.28

2.29

Vivace

2.30

Andante cantabile

2.31

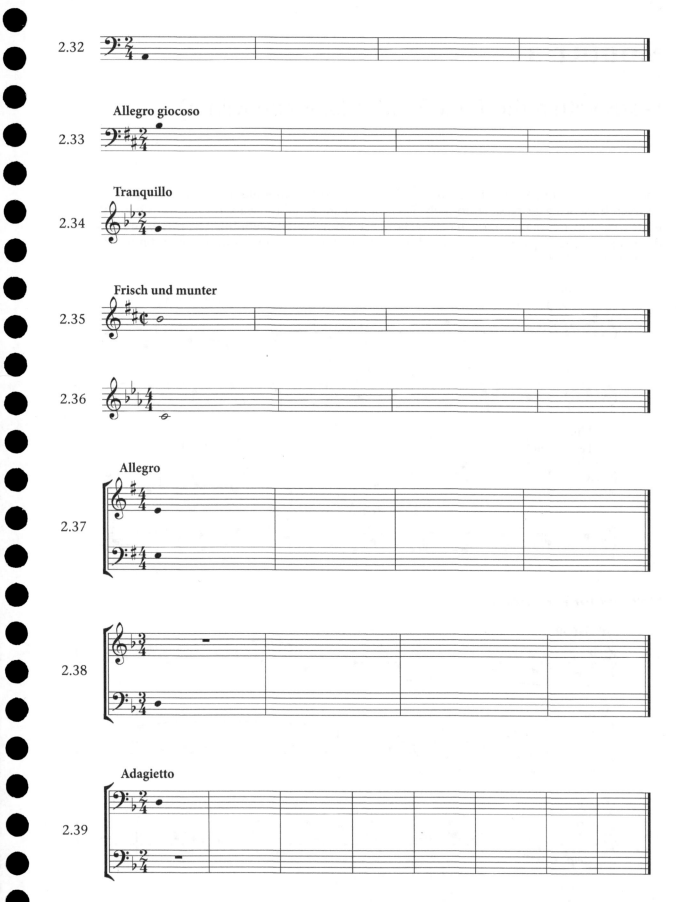

MODULE 3

Leaps within the Tonic Triad (Major and Minor)

The tonic triad consists of scale degrees $\hat{1}$, $\hat{3}$, and $\hat{5}$, and this module focuses on the ability to leap between these scale degrees comfortably. Example 3.1 shows all the leaps that are possible within the tonic triad and are smaller than an octave, both ascending and descending. Use this example to practice singing these leaps accurately. Which tonic-triad leaps are different in major and minor? Which leaps are the same?

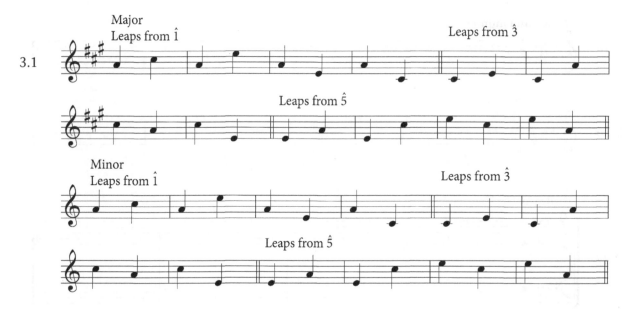

Melodies for Performance

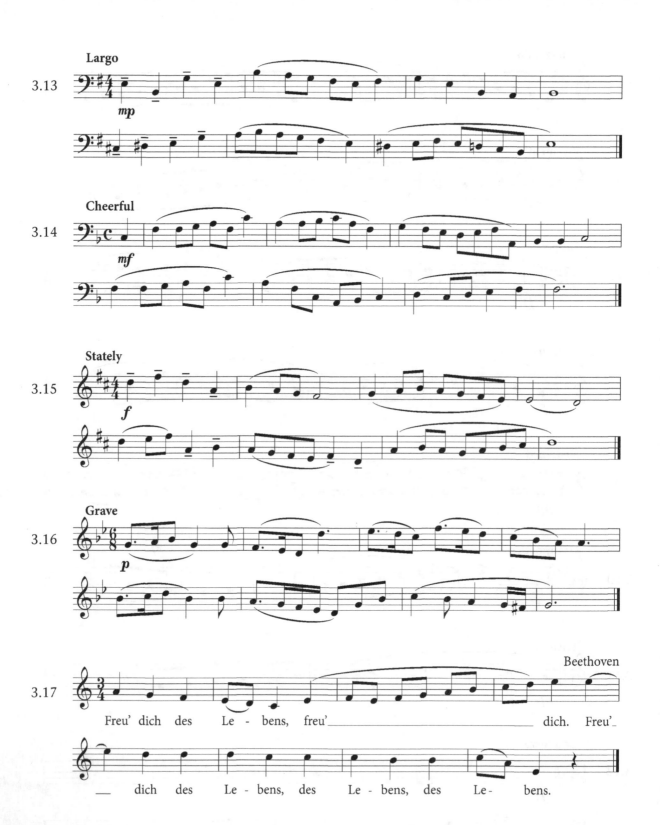

Leise   Schumann

3.18

Ich will mei-ne See - le tau - chen in den Kelch der Li - lie hin - ein,   die

Li - lie soll klin - gend hau - chen esin Lied von der Lieb -sten   mein.

3.19   Anonymous

1.)   2.)   3.)

E - go sum pau - per.   Ni -hil ha - be - o.   Cor me -um da - bo.

3.20   Praetorius

1.)   2.)   3.)   4.)

5.)   6.)   7.)   8.)

3.21   Luigi Cherubini

1.)   2.)   3.)

Sostenuto ed espressivo

3.22

1.)   2.)   3.)   4.)

pp   *p*

♪. = 104

3.23

1.)   2.)   3.)

mf

4.)   5.)

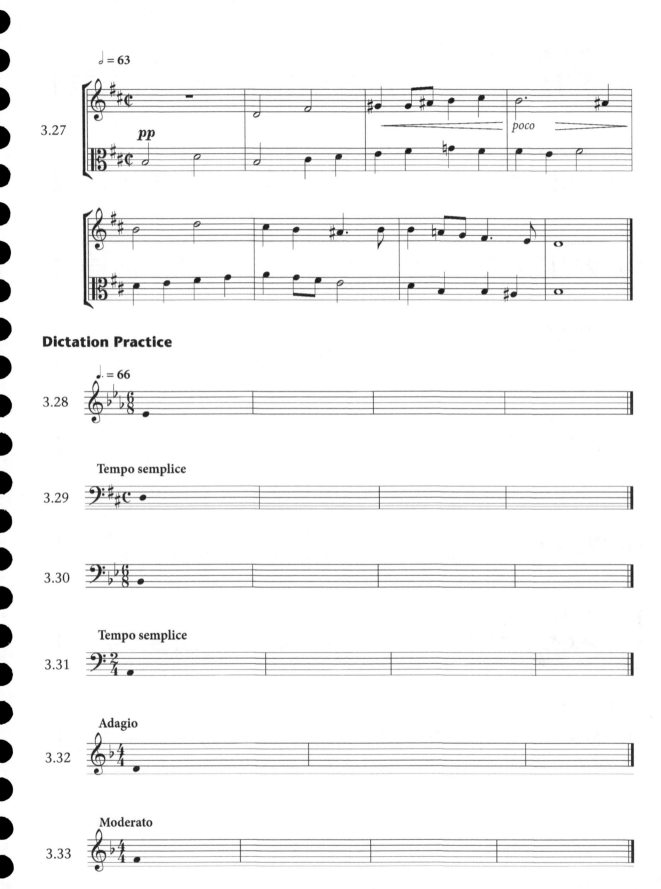

Dictation Practice

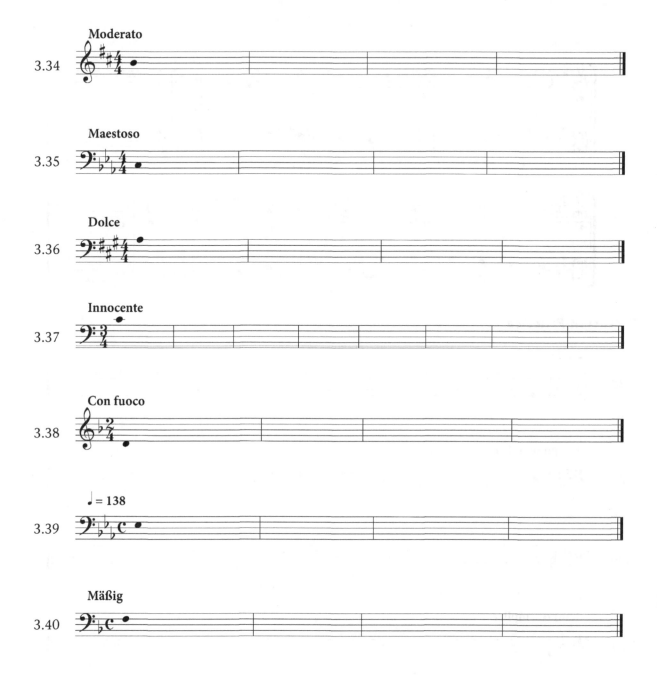

3.42

Gemütlich

3.43

Con brio

MODULE 4

Leaps within the Dominant (Seventh) and vii°

Example 4.1 shows the leaps that are introduced in this module. Because four scale degrees are involved, there are more leaps to learn than there were in Module 3. Be sure to establish a solid sense of tonic before working on this exercise, and feel free to refresh your tonic should it slip from memory.

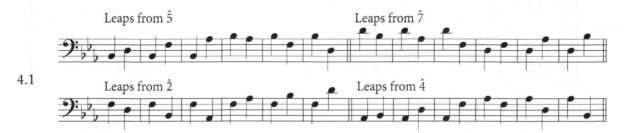

4.1

Since the leading-tone is typically raised in minor, there will be no difference between the dominant triad in major and in minor in this module.

Melodies for Performance

Germany

4.19 Wir sing - en jetzt ein Trul - la - la, trul - la - la, trul - la - la, Wir

sing a lit - tle trul - la - la, Trul - la - la.

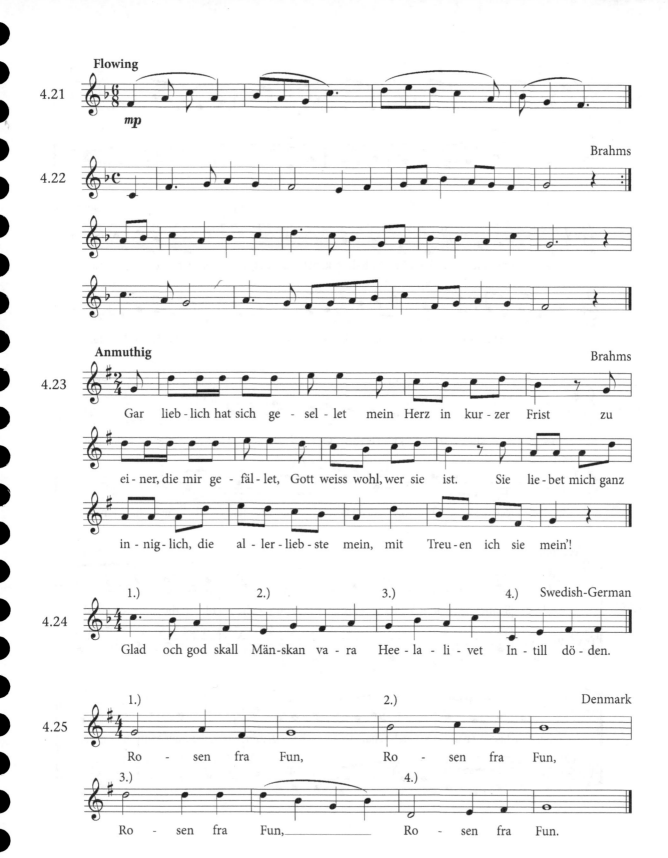

4.21 **Flowing** _mp_

4.22 Brahms

4.23 **Anmuthig** Brahms

Gar lieb-lich hat sich ge - sel-let mein Herz in kur-zer Frist zu

ei - ner, die mir ge - fäl-let, Gott weiss wohl, wer sie ist. Sie lie-bet mich ganz

in - nig-lich, die al-ler-lieb-ste mein, mit Treu-en ich sie mein'!

4.24 1.) 2.) 3.) 4.) Swedish-German

Glad och god skall Män-skan va-ra Hee-la-li-vet In-till dö-den.

4.25 1.) 2.) Denmark

Ro - sen fra Fun, Ro - sen fra Fun,

3.) 4.)

Ro - sen fra Fun,_____ Ro - sen fra Fun.

Dictation Practice

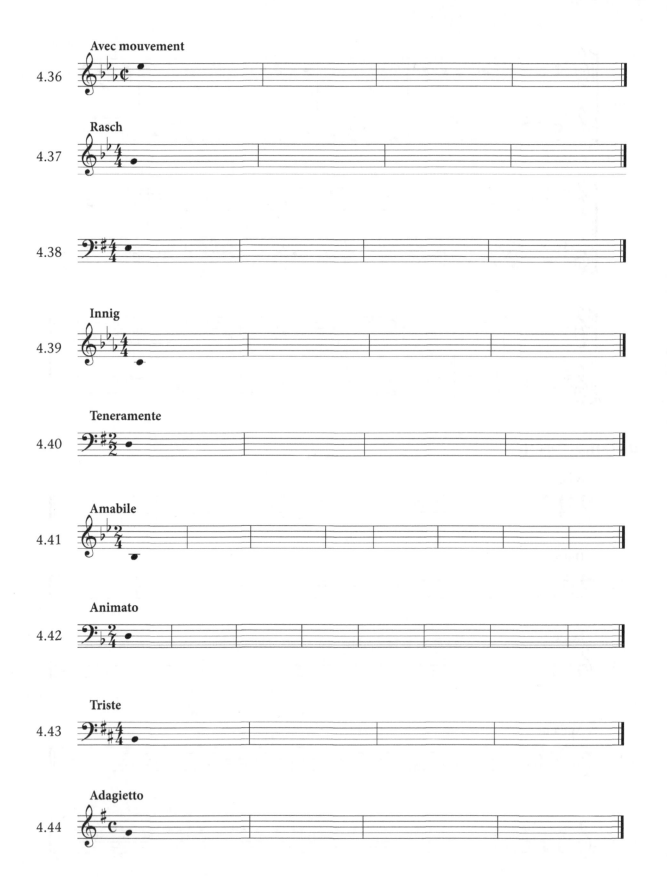

MODULE 5

Further Diatonic Leaps

In this module you will begin leaping freely between various scale degrees, including the one you have yet to encounter as either the origin or the goal of a leap: $\hat{6}$. At this point you should be comfortable with leaps of various sizes, both up and down, and you should be acquiring a strong familiarity with each scale degree.

Melodies for Performance

"Nessun dorma" Turandot

Andante sostenuto   Puccini

5.11

Ma il mio mi-ste-ro è chioso in   me;   il no-me mio nes-sun sa -prà! No, no! Sul-la tua

boc - ca lo di - rò_____ quan-do la lu – ce splen-de - rà!

Lento ma non troppo   Chopin

5.12

Andantino   Kling

5.13

Wales

5.14

Allegro giocoso

5.15

5.16 Ritmico

5.17 Pas vite

d'Indy

Quand la ber - gè - re vat - aux champs Qouand la ber - gè - re vat - aux___

champs, Tout en fi - lant sa cou - lon - net - te, Tout___ en - gar

dant ses jo - lis blancs mout - tons Tout le long de la ri - viè - re.

5.18

Petzold

5.19

Hilton

1.) Come, fol - low, fol - low, fol - low, fol - low fol - low, fol - low me.

2.) Whi - ther shall I fol - low, fol - low, fol - low, Whi - ther shall I fol - low, fol - low thee?

3.) To the green - wood, to the green - wood, to the green - wood, green - wood tree.

Israel

5.20

Toem- baï, toem- baï, toem- baï, toem- baï, toem- baï, toem- baï, toem- baï, tra la la, la la la la la, la la la la la la. Tra la la la la la la la la la la la la la la la la.

Mässig

5.21

mf

Praetorius

5.22

Ju – bi – la – te, De – o, Ju –bi –la –te, De – o, Al – le –lu – jah!

Deciso

5.23

ff

Allegro deciso

5.24

C. Schumann

5.25

Wenn ich ein Vög- lein wär und auch zwei Flü- gel hätt, flög ich zu dir, zu dir.

Freudig   Schubert

5.26

Grü-ner wird die Au,   und der Him-mel blau!   Schwal-ben keh - ren

wid - der   und die Erst - lings - lie - der   klei - ner Vö - ge -

lein   zwit-schern durch___ den Hain.

Dictation Practice

Kraft

5.27

Andante piacevole

5.28

♩. = 116

5.29

Etwas gedehnt

5.30

Bewegt

5.31

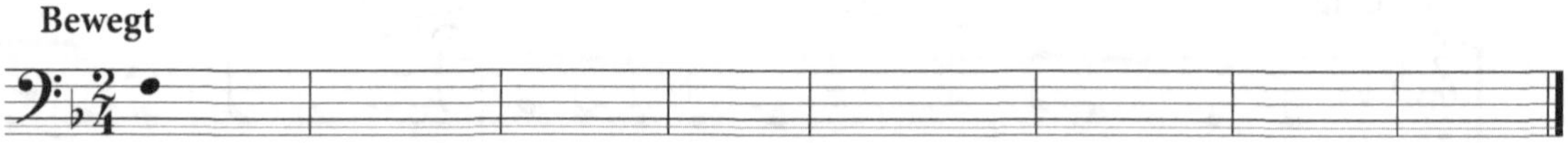

Allegro assai

5.32

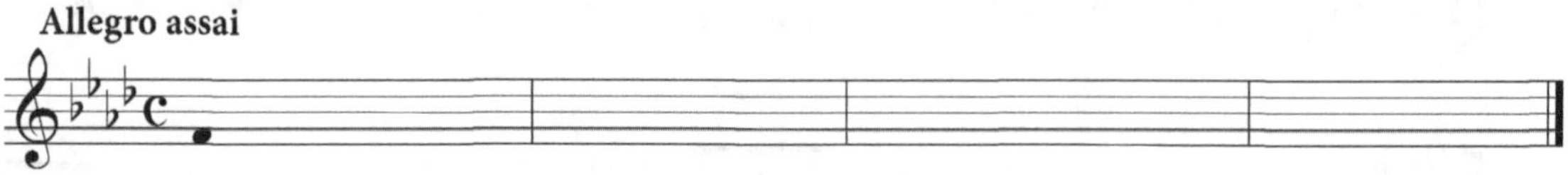

Fliessend

5.33

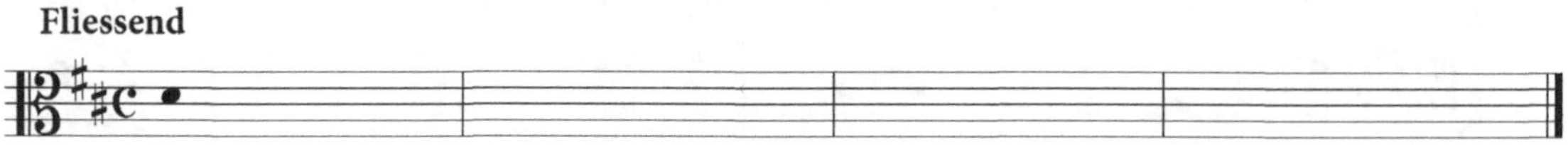

♩ = 104

5.34

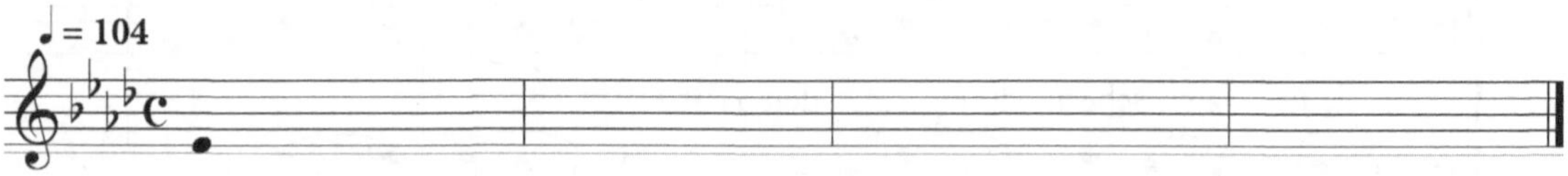

Lebhaft

5.35

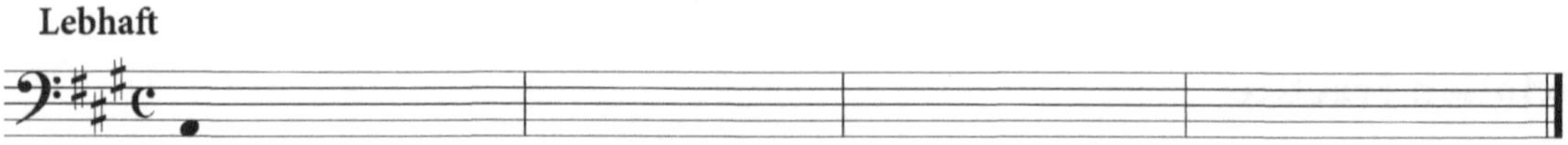

Amabile

5.36

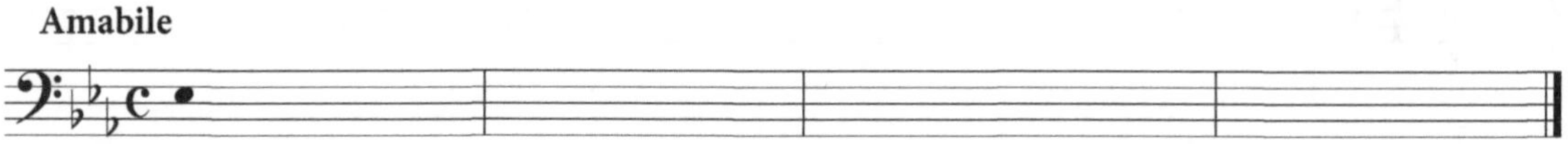

Ruhig

5.37

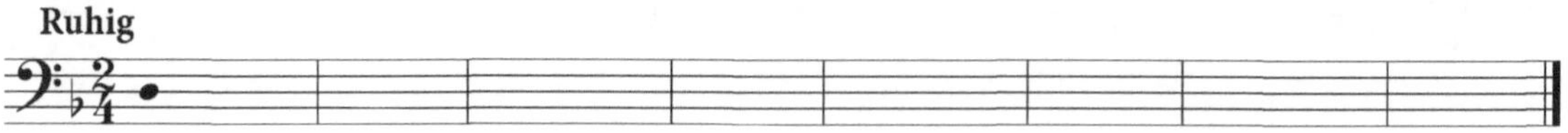

Teneramente

5.38

Vivo

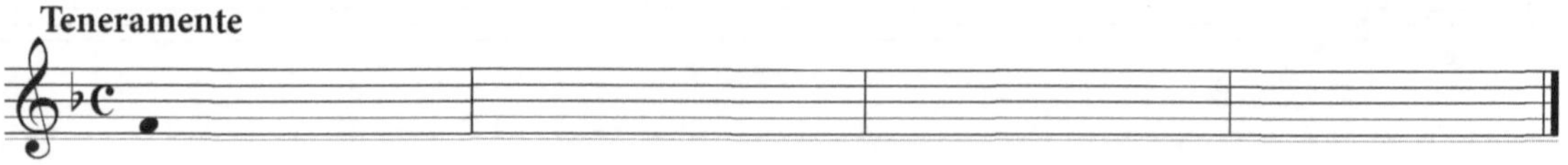

5.39

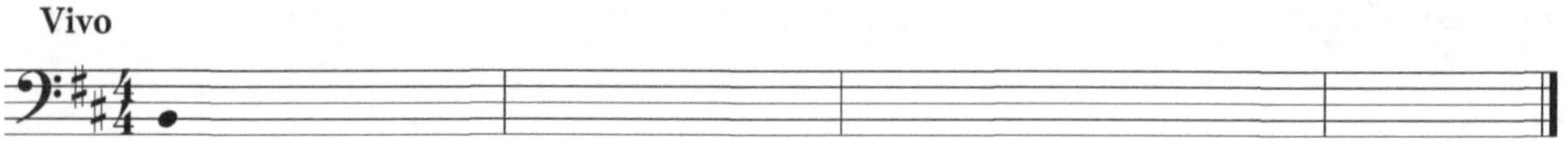

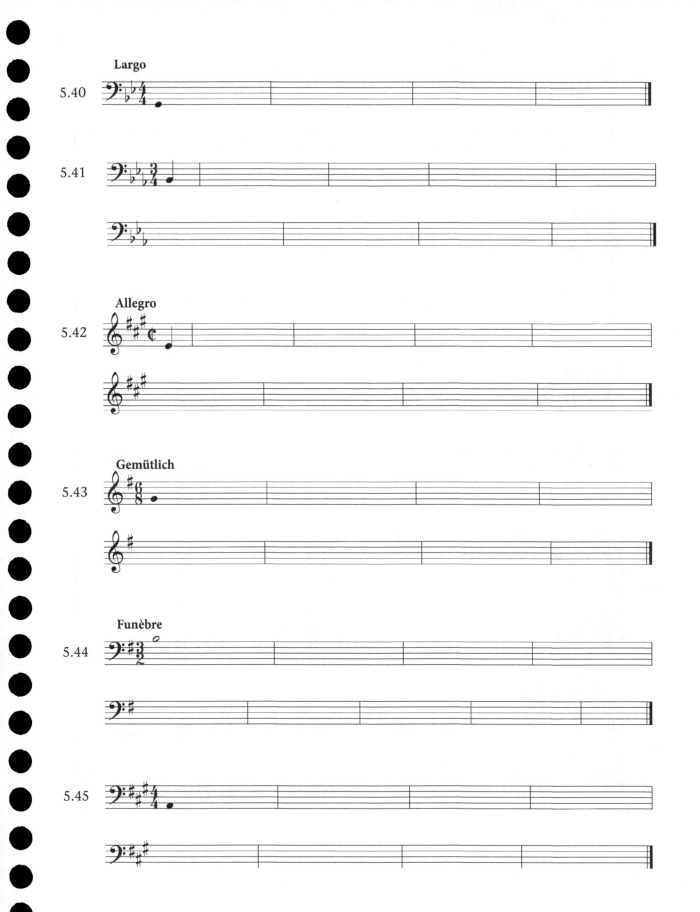

MODULE 6

Stepwise Chromatic Tones

In previous modules you have only seen accidentals when dealing with the raised and lowered versions of $\hat{6}$ and $\hat{7}$ in the minor mode. In this module accidentals can and will appear in both major and minor keys, and on virtually any scale degree. The notes that are altered by accidentals will be referred to as *chromatic*, as opposed to those that are diatonic (those seven pitches that are specified by the key signature). Because this is an introduction to chromaticism, the chromatic pitches in this module will be restricted to those that are both approached and left by step. Example 6.1 includes one such pitch, a chromatic neighbor tone. As you can see, the defining feature of the chromatic neighbor tone is that it embellishes a diatonic note by stepping away from it and then right back.

6.1

chromatic
neighbor tone

The other possibility for stepwise chromaticism is the chromatic passing tone, which comes in two varieties, both of which can be seen in Example 6.2. In the first type of chromatic passing tone, the chromatic pitch lies between two adjacent diatonic pitches; F♯ passes between F♮ and G, which are adjacent scale degrees in the key of C major. In the second type, a diatonic pitch is replaced by its own chromatic variant; B♭ replaces the diatonic B♮ in passing motion between C and A.

6.2

As you practice the examples in this module, keep in mind that all three of these chromatic tones serve to embellish an otherwise diatonic line. This means that if you encounter difficulty with a chromatic pitch you can always refer back to a diatonic pitch that is nearby in order to regain your sense of tonic and your location within the scale.

Melodies for Performance

Allegro con brio

6.3

Munter

6.4

Brisk

6.5

Allegro molto

6.6

Andante tranquillo   Mendelssohn

6.7

6.8   Beethoven

6.9   Maker

For all the blue of sky and sea, For flash of sea - gulls' wing, For wind and wave and spray flung free For stars that will our guide e'er be, Our thanks to thee we sing.

Allegretto (♪ = 138)   Lemoine

6.10

poco rit.

6.11   Schumann

Wenn ich früh in den Gar - ten geh', in mei - nem grü - nen Hut, ist mein er - ster Ge - dan - ke, was nun__ mein Lieb - ster thut, ist mein er - ster Ge - dan - ke, was nun mein Lieb - ster thut.

6.12

England

Oh, Mis-tress Sha-dy,___ she is a la-dy.___ She has a daugh-ter___whom I a-

dore.___ Each night I court her,___ I mean the daugh-ter,___ Ev'-ry

Sun-day, Mon-day, Tues-day, We'n's-day, Thurs-day, Fri-day,

Sat-ur-day, Sun-day af-ter-noon at half past four.___

Adagio e sostenuto

6.13

Kuhlau

p con espress.

p

cresc.

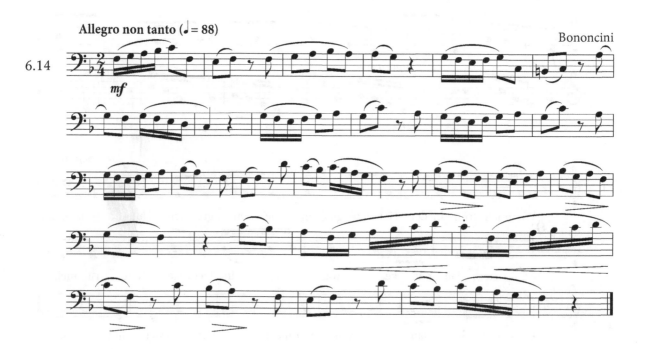

Allegro non tanto (♩ = 88)

6.14

Bononcini

mf

Lieblich — Schubert

6.19

Dictation Practice

6.20 ♩ = 138

6.21 **Allegro deciso**

6.22 **Andante con moto**

6.23 **Moderato cantabile**

Allegro con spirito

6.24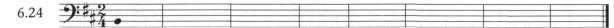

Somber

6.25

Allegretto

6.26

Adagietto

6.27

Sustained

6.28

Cheerful

6.29

Swaying

6.30

Lebhaft

6.31

Frisch und munter

6.32

Andante cantabile

6.33

Allegro

6.34

Allegro moderato

6.35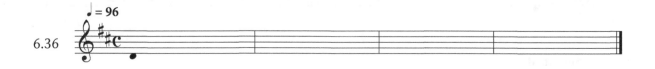

♩ = 96

6.36

Dolcissimo

6.37

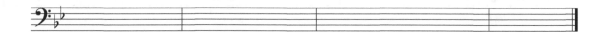

Somber

6.38

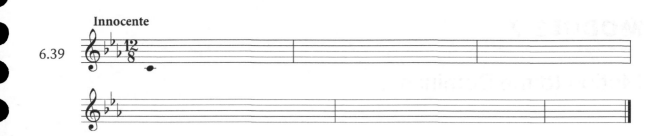

6.39

MODULE 7

Motion to the Dominant

The two most common points of harmonic repose (i.e., cadential goals) in tonal music are I and V. For this reason melodies often come to pause on scale degrees $\hat{1}$ and $\hat{3}$, which are the root and third of the I chord, and on $\hat{5}$, $\hat{7}$, and $\hat{2}$, which are the root, third, and fifth of the V chord. This module draws special attention to melodic arrivals on members of the V chord, some of which are temporary, occurring roughly at the midway point of a melody, and some of which are more final sounding, occurring at the end of a melody.

In addition, the study of chromatic tones continues by focusing on a specific chromatic pitch, $\sharp\hat{4}$, which is a tendency tone that leads strongly to $\hat{5}$. The motion of $\sharp\hat{4}$ to $\hat{5}$ mimics the resolution of $\hat{7}$ to $\hat{1}$, a melodic feature that is so powerful that it can be chromatically applied to other scale degrees. The melodies in this module employ $\sharp\hat{4}$ as a temporary leading-tone to $\hat{5}$. This means that you will on occasion hear the dominant scale degree as the new tonic, either temporarily or permanently. Example 7.1 includes a motion to the dominant and shows how one might temporarily think of the scale degrees involved in the melodic approach to $\hat{5}$ in either the home key of A major, or in the key of the dominant: E major.

A weak or temporary motion to $\hat{5}$ is sometimes called a tonicization, as opposed to a proper modulation, which is a stronger motion to the dominant in which the music convincingly changes keys. To qualify as a true modulation several factors have to be considered, including the harmonic support, the length of the passage that emphasizes $\hat{5}$, and so on. Depending on the solmization system you use, these moments can present a challenge in that you will want your syllables to match your musical experience. If $\hat{5}$ doesn't sound like $\hat{5}$ any more, but has taken on the quality of $\hat{1}$ (even if only for the time being), do you still want to call it $\hat{5}$?

In addition to encouraging you to think about $\sharp\hat{4}$ as a temporary $\hat{7}$, this module will also include leaps into and away from $\sharp\hat{4}$.

Melodies for Performance

Ruhig, mässig — Schubert

7.2
Gross und_ ro-thent flam-met_ schwe-bet noch die_ Sonn' am Him-mels-rand, und auf_ blauen Wo gen_ ba-bet noch ihr_ Ab-glanz bis zum Strand.

Etwas geschwind — Schubert

7.3
Lei - ser, lei - ser, klei - ne Lau - te, flü - stre, was___ ich dir ver-trau-te, dort zu je - nem Fen - ster hin!

Allegretto (♪ = 138) — Rod

7.4
f *mf* *cresc.* *f*

Froh und frei — Schubert

7.5
Auf ho hem Ber - ges-rü - cken, wo frisch-er al - les grünt, in's Land hi-nab zu bli - cken, das ne-bel-leicht zer - rinnt, er - freut den Al - pen - jä - ger, er - freut den Al - pen - jä - ger.

Moderato

Mozart

7.14

A - pri - teun po' quegl' oc - chi, Uo - mi - niin - cau - tie schioc - chi, Guar

da - te que - ste fem - mi - ne, guar - da - te co - sa son, guar

da - te co - sa son, guar - da - te, guar - da - te co - sa son!

Allegro moderato

Mozart

7.15

Un mo - to di gio - ja mi sen - to nel pet - to, che an - nun - zia__ di - let - te__ in__

mez - zo il ti - mor! Spe - riam che in con - ten - to fi - ni - sca l'af - fan - no, non

sem - pre, non sem - pre é ti - ran - no il__ fa - to ed a - mor,

il__ fa - to ed a - mor.__ Un__ mo - to di gio - ja mi

sen - to nel pet - to, che an - nun - zia__ di - let - to__ in mez - zo il til - mor.

Schubert

7.16

7.17 **Lebhaft und gut gelaunt**   Schumann

Gu-ten A-bend, mein Schatz, gu-ten A - ben, mein Kind, gu-ten A - bend, mein

Kind! Ich komm aus Lieb zu__ dir, ach, mach mir auf die_ Tür, mach mir auf die

Tür, mach mir auf, mach mir auf, mach mir auf__ die Tür!

7.18 **Andante**   Maylath

7.19 **Dolce**   Scarlatti

7.20 **Adagio**   J. S. Bach

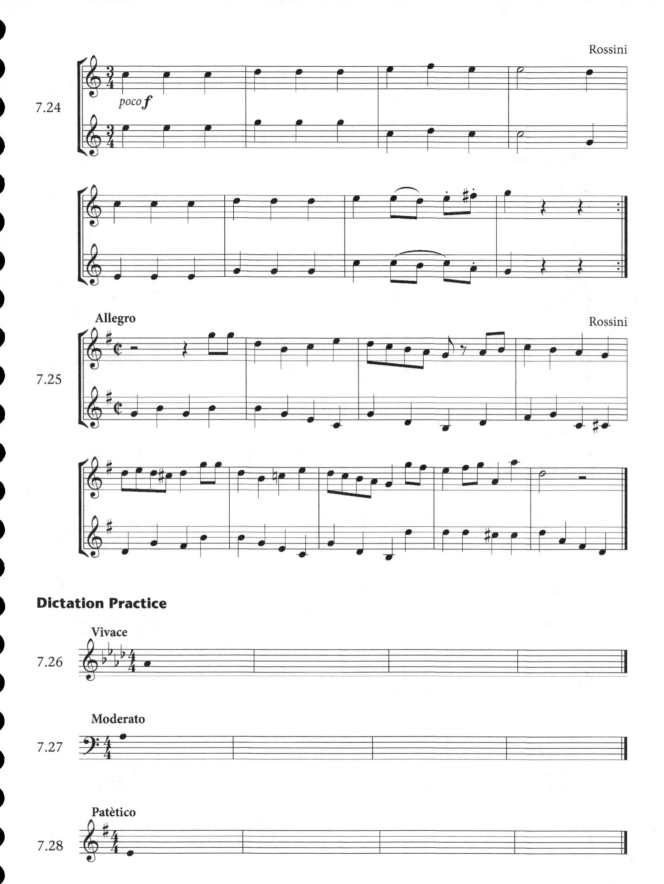

Dictation Practice

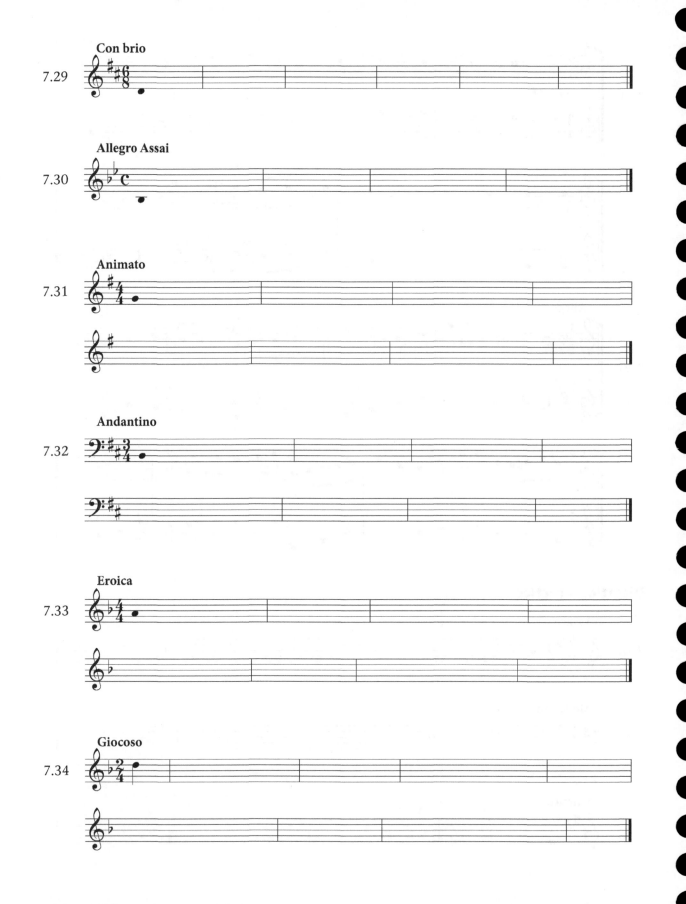

7.40

MODULE 8

Leaps to and from Chromatic Tones

In this module the study of chromatic tones continues with leaps into and away from various chromatically altered scale degrees. In Example 8.1 the same chromatic pitch (♯2̂) is approached first by step and then by skip. In both cases the chromatic pitch resolves by step up to diatonic 3̂.

8.1

If you are having trouble singing a chromatic pitch correctly, it often helps to revert back to the stepwise motion introduced in Module 6. You can do this by singing the diatonic pitch that the chromatic pitch resolves to, *then* singing the chromatic pitch (like a neighbor tone) until you are sufficiently familiar with it to go back and sing the excerpt as written. Another technique is to sing the diatonic version of a chromatic pitch, then determine what its raised or lowered version should sound like.

Melodies for Performance

Ruhig

Schubert

8.10

Heins

8.11

There's a voice in the wil-der-ness cry - ing, A call from the ways un -

trod: Pre - pare in the des - ert a high - way, A

high - way for our God! The val - leys shall be ex - alt - ed, The

loft - y hills brought low; Make straight all the crook ed

plac - es, Where the Lord our___ God may go!

Arne

8.12

8.13

Anonymous

Come a - way, fel-low sai-lors, come a - way, your an - chors be weigh-ing, Time and
tide will ad - mit no_ de - lay-ing; Take a booz-y short leave of your nymphs of the
shore, And si - lence their mourn-ing With vows of re - turn-ing, But nev - er in -
tend-ing to vis - it them more, no ne-ver in - tend-ing to vis - it them
more, no nev-er, no nev-er in - tend-ing to_ vis - it them more!

Langsam

8.14

Schubert

Lebhaft

8.15

1.)

2.)

3.)

4.)

8.18

Täusch mich nicht, ver-laß mich nicht, du weißt nicht, wie lieb__ ich dich hab'

lieb' du mich__ wie ich dich,__ dann strömt Got-tes Huld auf dich her-ab!

Brahms

8.19 **Maestoso** (♩ = 80)

Righini

8.20 **Andantino** ♪. = 60

Paisiello

Nel cor più non mi sen-to bril-lar la____ gio-ven-tù; ca-

gion del mio__ tor-men-to, a-mor, sei col-pa tu. Mi piz-zi-chi, mi

stuz-zi chi, mi pun-gi-chi, mi mas-ti-chi; che co-sa è que-sto ahi

mè?____ pie-tà, pie-tà, pie-tà!__ a-mo-re è un-cer-to

che,_____ che di-spe-rar__ mi fa.

8.21

Du hei - lig, glü - hend A - bend roth! der Him - mel will__ in

Glanz zer rin-nen, der Him - mel will in Glanz__ zer__ rin-nen.

Dictation Practice

Berceuse

8.22

Doux

8.23

Breit

8.24

Amabile

8.25

Tempo comodo

8.26

Piacevole

8.27

Gioviale

8.28

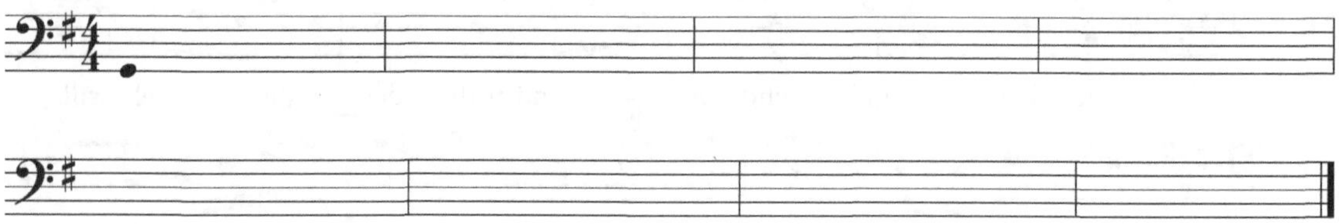

Rasch

8.29

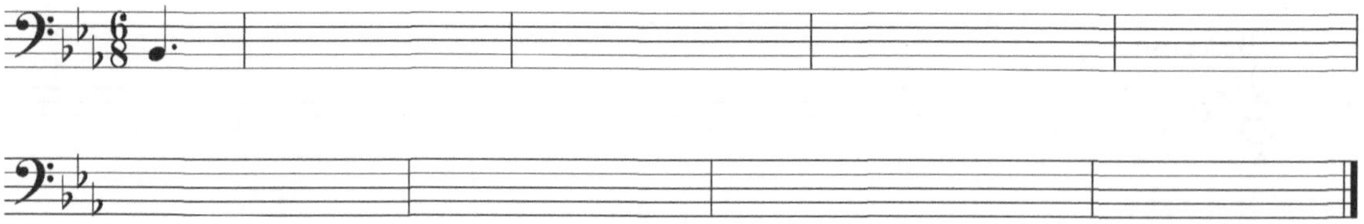

Moderato

8.30

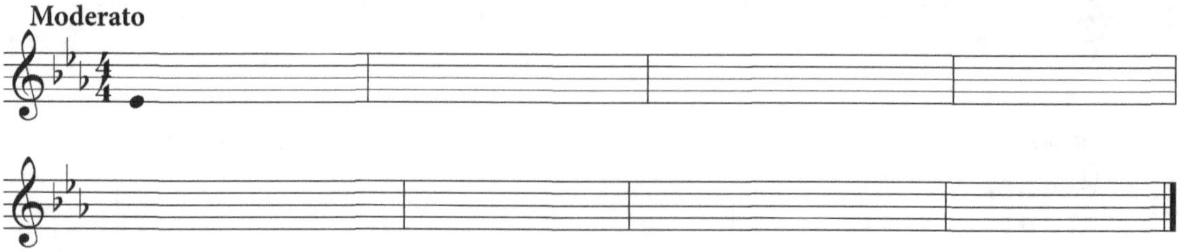

Lustig

8.31

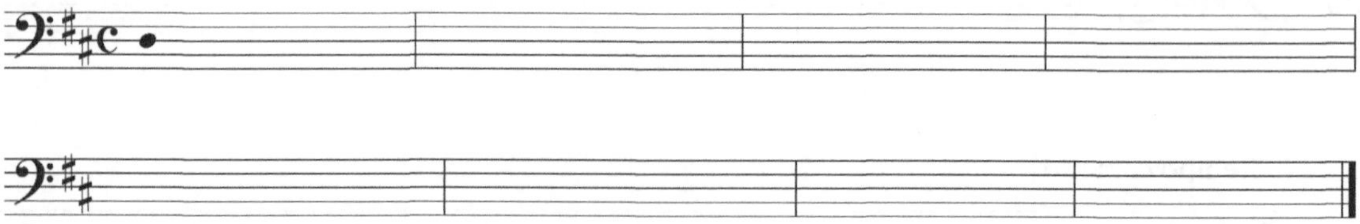

Lebhaft

8.32

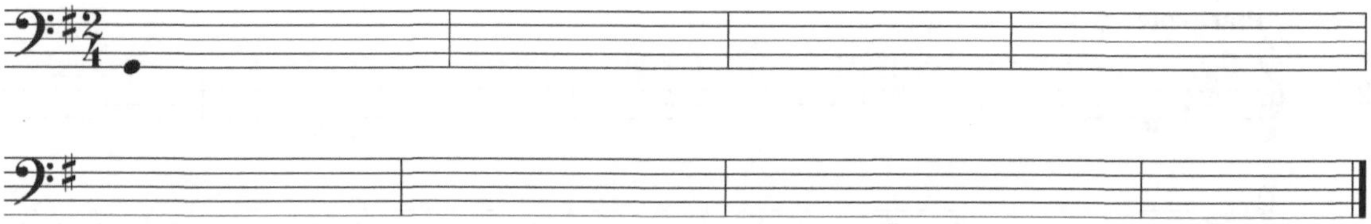

Pomposo

8.33

Andantino

8.34

Vivace

8.35

Marcia

8.36

Doux

8.37

MODULE 9

Modulation to Closely Related Keys

In Module 7 you practiced singing and hearing musical passages in which the role of tonic shifts from a starting note to its dominant. In this module such shifts will take place from a starting note to any of its closely related keys.

Closely related keys are those that have either the same key signature or one with only one accidental different from the key signature of origin. For example, if the overall (or global) key of a piece is D major, the major keys that are closely related are G and A because the former has one fewer sharp and the latter one more sharp. The minor keys that are closely related to D major are B minor, E minor, and F♯ minor. Example 9.1 shows a segment of the circle of fifths, including the keys that are closely related to D major. Why is it that C major and A minor are *not* closely related to D major?

9.1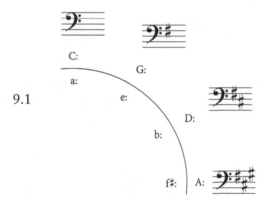

Notice also that all six of the tonal centers represented by the keys that are closely related to D major are also scale degrees in that key: D, E, F♯, G, A, and B. Furthermore, D major, E minor, F♯ minor, G major, A major, and B minor are all diatonic triads in D major.

As you sing, you will have to decide whether you should switch solmization syllables (depending on the system you are using) and, if so, where. These decisions represent a genuine leap in your sight-singing because they require you to evaluate the music in a much more sophisticated way than before. Rather than merely reacting to the musical surface you will now need to think about what keys are being implied, and you will be forced on occasion to embrace the ambiguity of a passage that could just as easily be in one key as in the next. Musical sensitivity and a willingness to experiment with different options will serve you well as you study the performance of modulations.

Melodies for Performance

9.2

Heimlich und zierlich bewegt

Brahms

9.8

Feins lieb - chen, du sollst mir nich bar - fuß

gehn, du zer trittst dir die zar - ten Füß - lein schön.

Largo

9.9

mp

Majestic

9.10

ff

Fast

9.11

f

Léger

9.12

mp

Allegretto vivo

mf

Delibes

9.13

Bon - jour, Su - zon, ma fleur des bois!_____ Es - tu tou jours la plus jo - li - e?

Je re - viens tel que tu me vois,_____ D'un grand vo - yage en I - ta - li - e.

Du pa - ra - dis j'ai fait le tour._____ J'ai fait des vers, j'ai fait l'a - mour._____

her' - ge Jun - ge der mir so lieb, ist ü - ber die Ber - ge weird hin - ans.

Dictation Practice

Affettuoso

9.27

p

Largo

9.28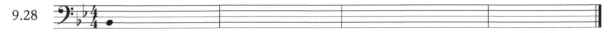

Allegretto

9.29

Allegro giocoso

9.30

Allegro moderato

9.31

Allegretto

9.32

9.33

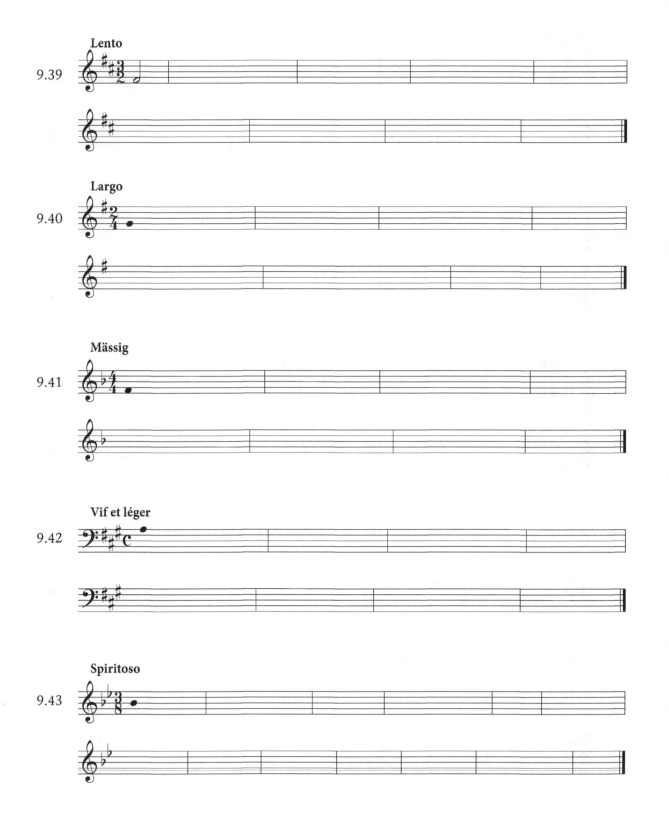

MODULE 10

Advanced Chromaticism

The purpose of this module is to reinforce skills acquired in earlier modules in a more challenging context.

Melodies for Performance

10.1 Allegretto (♪ = 138) — Lemoine

10.2 — Schubert

Wenn mich ein - sam Lüf - te fä - cheln,   muss_ ich lä   cheln,

wie ich_ kin-disch tän - delnd ko - se   mit____ der Ro - se.

10.3 Lustig im Tempo und keck im Ausdruck — Mahler

10.4 Adagio espressivo — Brahms

Mässig   Schubert

10.5

Wo ein treus Her — ze In Lie - be ver- geht, Da wel - ken die Li - lien Auf

je — dem Beet; Da muß in die Wol- ken Der Voll - mond gehn, Da-

mit sei - ne Trä - nen Die Mensch - en___ nicht sehn.

Alla Marcia   Mahler

10.6

                                                                           J. S. Bach

10.7

Wie vorher   Mahler

10.8

10.22

Brahms

10.23

Dun - kel, wie dun - kel in Wald und in Feld! A - bend schon ist es, nun

schwei - get die Welt. Nir - gend noch Licht und nir - gend noch

Rauch, ja, und die Ler - che sie schwei - get nun auch.

Langsam, wehmüthig

Schubert

10.24

Guess, lie - ber Mond, geuss dei - ne Sil - ber flim - mer durch

die - ses Bu - cheng - rün, wo Phan - ta - sien__ und

Traum - ge - stal - ten im - mer vor mir - nor - ü - ber flieh'n!

Etwas langsamer

Mahler

10.25

pp

p

Dictation Practice

Largo con affetto

10.30

10.31

10.32

10.33

10.34

10.35

Jaunty

10.36

En allant

10.37

Modéré

10.43

Bewegt

10.44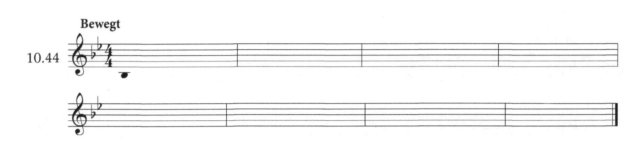

Con brio

10.45

Gemütlich

10.46

Fröhlich

10.47

MODULE 11

Modulation to Distantly Related Keys

The melodies in this module modulate to keys that are distantly related, offering a much larger number of possibilities. By now you should be rather familiar with the challenges and pitfalls associated with modulation, but it is nevertheless worth mentioning the three most important questions when sight-reading a modulating melody:

1. What key does it start in?
2. What key does it end in?
3. Where does the modulation actually happen?

If you can answer these questions, then you are almost sure to succeed in your interpretation.

Melodies for Performance

Drammatico

11.17

Dictation Practice

Mässig

11.18

♩ = 69

11.19

Adagio

11.20

♩ = 108

11.21

Marcia

11.22

Larghetto

11.23

MODULE 12

Pentatonic and Diatonic Modes

Pentatonic Modes

As its name reveals, a pentatonic scale has five scale degrees. The most common pentatonic scale can be thought of as a subset of the diatonic collection, as shown in Example 12.1. This collection is sometimes referred to as the major pentatonic scale, although because it is so very common it is often simply called the pentatonic scale. Notice that the two scale degrees that are missing from this pentatonic scale are the two tendency tones that were mentioned in the introduction to Module 1.

12.1

Example 12.2 shows an alternative rotation of the same five notes, now with A as the implied tonic. This collection is sometimes referred to as the minor pentatonic scale.

12.2

Other rotations of this pitch collection are also possible, as are pentatonic scales that are made up of altogether different intervals, but the major and minor pentatonic scales will be used exclusively in this module because they are so common.

Diatonic Modes

The melody in Example 12.3 unequivocally points to A as the tonic, but has the key signature of neither A major nor A minor. Rather, this melody is in the Mixolydian mode.

12.3

There are seven diatonic modes for every key signature, and there are two ways of modeling the modes. The first way, which is historically accurate, is to list the modes in ascending order along the notes of a given diatonic collection. For example, with no sharps or flats in the key signature the major scale, which is the Ionian mode, has C for a tonic. With the same open key signature, the scale that has D for a tonic is the Dorian mode. Example 12.4 provides a complete listing of the modes in this fashion.

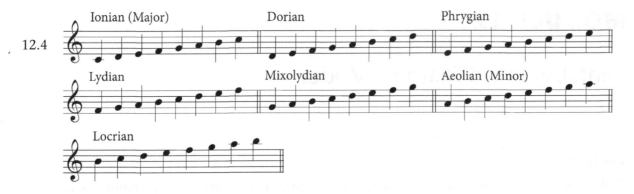

For every key signature it would be possible to create a graphic such as 12.4 and in every case the order of the modes would be the same.

The second way of organizing the diatonic modes is to maintain a consistent tonic and alter the key signature. In Example 12.5 the first line has modes with major 3rd scale degrees and the modes in the second line have minor 3rd scale degrees. Notice also that these scales are arranged so that their implied key signatures are in circle-of-fifths order, resulting in a smooth progression from one sharp to five flats, all while maintaining C as the tonic.

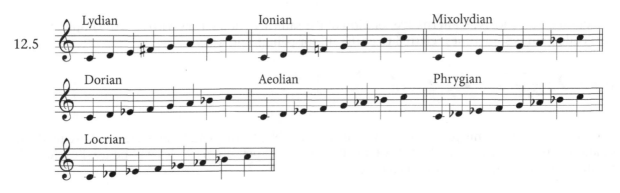

This second way of organizing the modes makes it easy to see that Lydian is major with ♯4 and Mixolydian is major with ♭7. Also, Dorian is natural minor with ♯6 and Phrygian is natural minor with ♭2.

Finally, because of its lowered fifth scale degree the Locrian mode is not commonly encountered (except in Jazz), so it will not appear in this module.

Melodies for Performance

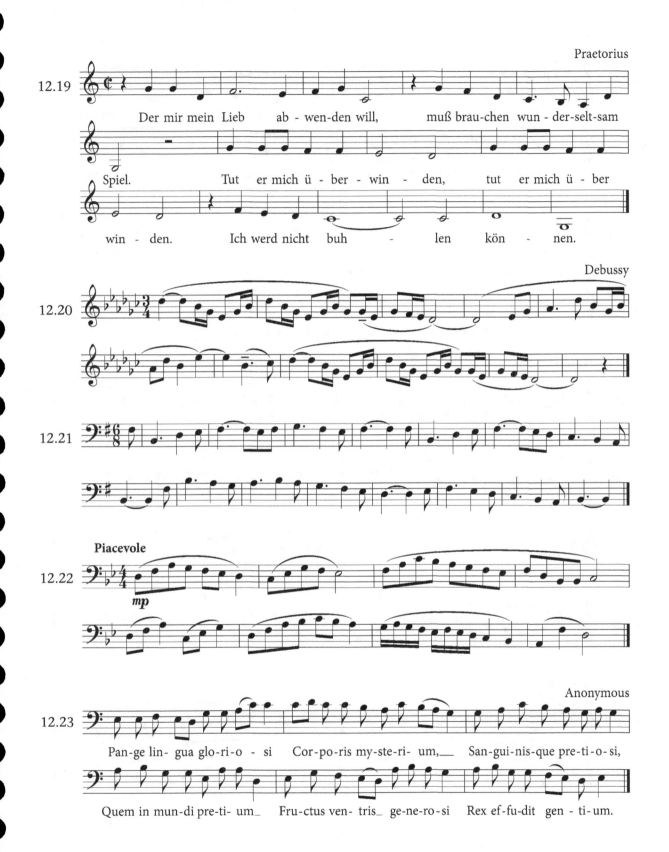

Lent   d'Indy

12.24 Ré-veil-lez vous, belle en - dor-mie, Ré-veil-lez vous, car - il est jou;

R - veil-lez vous belle en - dor-mie, Vous en-ten-drez par - ler de vous.

Anonymous

12.25 Pu-er na-tus in Beth-le-hem, a-le-lu-ia. Un-de gau-det Je-ru-sa-lem, a-le-lu-ia,

a-le-lu-ia! In cor-dis ju-bi-lo Chris-tum na-tum a-do-re-mus, cum no-vo can-ti-co.

Lento

12.26 1.)   2.)

12.27 1.)   2.)

f   3.)

12.28 1.)   2.)   3.)

p

♩. = 108 1.)

12.29

2.)

12.39 Moderato

Dictation Practice

12.40 Fliessend

12.41

12.42 Semplice

12.43 Moderato

MODULE 13

Other Modes

The whole-tone, octatonic, and hexatonic scales are sometimes collectively referred to as *synthetic* modes, a term with implications that are beyond the scope of this book. As its name suggests, the whole-tone scale consists entirely of whole-steps. Example 13.1 shows the only two transpositions of the scale, beginning somewhat arbitrarily on C and D♭. Any note in the whole-tone scale can be the tonic and because of its thoroughly consistent intervallic structure, all six rotations of the whole-tone scale sound the same. It is also possible—indeed, common—for the whole-tone scale to be employed in such a way that *no* pitch acts as tonic.

13.1

The octatonic scale consists of alternating whole-steps and half-steps. There are three unique transpositions of this scale, which is important for the purposes of composition and analysis, but for the purposes of performance it is equally important to note that there are just two unique rotations of the octatonic collection. Example 13.2 shows that one rotation begins with a half-step and the other begins with a whole-step. In this example, C was chosen as a starting note for convenience, but any note in either of these collections could just as easily be heard or employed as tonic, and, like the whole-tone scale, octatonic scales can be used without implying any single note as tonic. The octatonic scale is also known as the diminished scale, or the half-whole diminished scale.

13.2

half-step   whole-step

The hexatonic scale, sometimes called the augmented scale, consists of alternating half-steps and minor thirds (sometimes spelled enharmonically as an augmented second). Again, there are two rotations of the scale, both of which are shown in Example 13.3.

13.3

half-step   minor third

The acoustic scale can be thought of as a hybrid of the Lydian and Mixolydian modes in that it is a major scale with both ♯4̂ and ♭7̂, as shown in Example 13.4. Notice that the C acoustic scale is a rotation of the ascending G natural minor scale.

13.4

Melodies for Performance

The next three melodies use the whole-tone scale.

Pesante

13.5

13.6

Munter

13.7

The next three melodies use the octatonic scale.

Giocoso

13.8

Frisch

13.9

Gracieux

13.10

The next three melodies use the hexatonic scale.

The following melodies use the acoustic scale.

Dictation Practice

The next three melodies use the whole-tone scale.

13.17

13.18

13.19

The next three melodies use the octatonic scale.

13.20

13.21

13.22

The next three melodies use the hexatonic scale.

13.23

Affettuoso

13.24

Tempo di menuetto

13.25

The next three melodies use the acoustic scale.

13.26

Tempo comodo

13.27

Amabile

13.28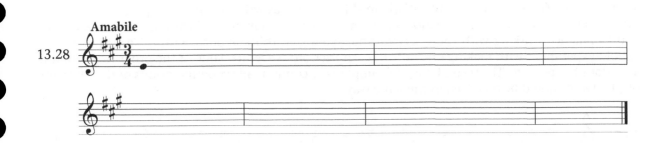

MODULE 14

Sets and 12-Tone Rows

This module is intended as a brief introduction to post-tonal aural skills. Example 14.1 is an étude on the singing of half-steps in tune. Be sure to transpose it to various pitch levels and try singing its exact inversion.

14.1

The next step is to begin working with motivic cells, or sets. The first line of Example 14.2 shows all six permutations of the set (014). Work on this example as written, then transpose it to begin on other pitches. Notice that these trichords are notated without a meter and without stems; this allows you to practice working with these sets without having to think about rhythm. Nevertheless, you should experiment with making one note of each trichord twice the value of the other two, working at various tempos, etc. The second line of Example 14.2 contains all six permutations of the inversion of (014) and should be practiced in the same way.

14.2

The two lines of Example 14.3 also feature the set class (014). The first line is made up of the same permutations as the first line of Example 14.2, in the same order, except that each permutation in Example 14.3 begins on the same note. The second line of Example 14.3 explores just one of the intervallic possibilities of (014) by inverting the thirds to sixths while preserving the half-step interval. Again, you should practice the trichords in Example 14.3 at various tempos and pitch levels.

14.3

In addition to (014), this module also features (016). Example 14.4 should be practiced in the same way as Examples 14.2 and 14.3.

14.4

The third and final trichord presented for study in this chapter is (026).

14.5

Melodies for Performance

The next three melodies are based on (014).

14.6

The next four melodies are based on (016).

The next three melodies are based on (026).

14.13 Con moto

14.14 Allegro assai

14.15 Andantino

The 12-tone row was one of the most influential musical ideas of the twentieth century. In short, the goal of the row is to cycle through all 12 of the pitches in the chromatic scale.

The first part of this module introduced the idea of singing in a post-tonal context and in the course of studying the trichords (014), (016), and (026) you were introduced to every interval that is possible in chromatic space. The primary challenge when singing a 12-tone row relates to the length of the row and maintaining proper intonation throughout. You will need to check your accuracy frequently at first but will find that with practice it will improve significantly.

All the melodies in this chapter are derived from the following three rows. Practice each of these rows in preparation for singing the melodies that follow.

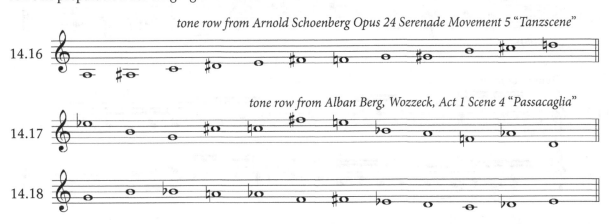

14.16 *tone row from Arnold Schoenberg Opus 24 Serenade Movement 5 "Tanzscene"*

14.17 *tone row from Alban Berg, Wozzeck, Act 1 Scene 4 "Passacaglia"*

14.18

Melodies for Performance

The next two melodies are based on the row given in Example 14.16.

The next two melodies are based on the row given in Example 14.17.

The next two melodies are based on the row given in Example 14.18.

Dictation Practice

The following melody is based on (014).

The following melody is based on (016).

The following melody is based on (026).

The following melody is based on the row given in Example 14.16.

The following melody is based on the row given in Example 14.17.

The following melody is based on the row given in Example 14.18.

PART 3

Harmony

MODULE 1

I(i) and V (1̂ and 5̂ in the Bass)

The Dictation Keys for Part 3 can be found at the end of the book (pages 327–384)

As you work through the examples in this module, it is important that you develop two habits right away. The first is the habit of paying special attention to the lowest sounding voice (the bass). The amateur music lover focuses his or her attention on the melody (the soprano), but the professional musician knows that the bass line provides a lot of important musical information. This module is your opportunity to focus on getting to know what scale degrees 1̂ and 5̂ sound like in the bass in a relatively simple context, which will be enormously helpful as the harmonic complexity mounts in the modules that follow.

The second habit to develop is that of checking your aural hunches against your knowledge about chords. For example, notice that the tonic triad (I) consists of scale degrees 1̂, 3̂, and 5̂, while V, the dominant, consists of 5̂, 7̂, and 2̂. This means that only I can support 1̂ and 3̂ in the melody, only V can support 7̂ and 2̂, but both I and V can support 5̂ (see Example 1.1).

This observation can confirm a hunch in either the bass or the soprano. For instance, suppose that you are sure you hear 3̂ in the soprano but aren't sure about the bass note that supports it. Example 1.1 clearly shows that I is the only harmony that can support 3̂, so it is clear what scale degree must be in the bass. You can also resolve a question about the soprano voice in the same way. For example, is it 2̂ or 3̂ that you are hearing in the soprano? If V is clearly in the bass it can only be 2̂. The application of knowledge to your aural impressions is difficult at first, but with time and practice it can become second nature.

Example 1.2 shows four typical voice leading patterns for the progression I–V–I. Again, pay special attention to the outer voices, soprano and bass.

In the minor mode the leading tone is almost always raised and the same voice leading patterns are typical.

1.3

Finally, remember that if you want to truly master the skill of transcription you will need to develop the habit of listening to music in a technical sense. Pay attention not only to the examples in this book, but also to the music you listen to outside of class, including pop music, movie soundtracks, or even the music you hear while shopping. Ask yourself technical questions. Is this major or minor? Which scale degrees do I hear? What harmonies are being employed? What is the meter? What instruments are playing? The world is full of transcription opportunities for the dedicated musician.

Examples for Performance

1.4

Note the passing tones in mm. 2–3 in the soprano and tenor lines.

1.5

Dictation Practice

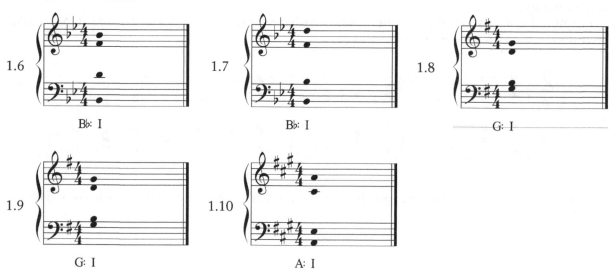

1.6   Bb: I

1.7   Bb: I

1.8   G: I

1.9   G: I

1.10   A: I

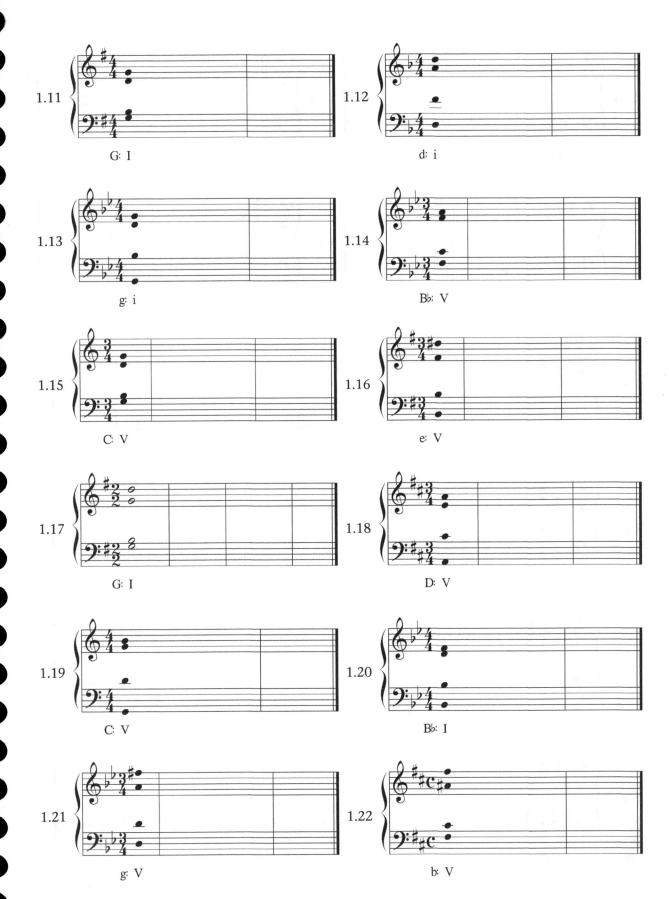

1.31   b: V

1.32   g: V

1.33   G: I

1.34   a: i

1.35   b: V

1.36   d: i

MODULE 2

IV(iv), ii⁶(°⁶), and ii (4̂ and 2̂ in the Bass)

The chords IV and ii are grouped together in this module because they have two scale degrees in common (4̂ and 6̂), and therefore sound very much alike. The I chord is tonic, the ever-present point of reference. The V chord serves as a convincing leading chord, different from and always pointing back to the tonic. IV and ii are the third pillar of diatonic harmony and most commonly function as pre-dominant chords—that is, chords that encourage us to anticipate the dominant chord that is likely to follow.

Just as I and V could support a limited number of scale degrees in the soprano, ii and IV are very strongly associated with scale degrees 4̂ and 6̂, neither of which are supported by I or V (see Example 2.1). On the other hand, 1̂ is supported by both IV and I, while 2̂ is supported by ii and V.

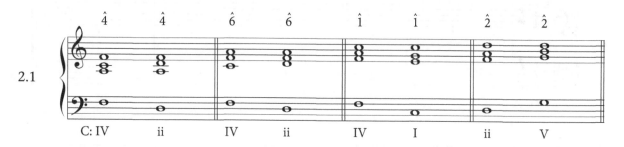

2.1

The Roman numeral for ii is written with lower case letters, reflecting the quality of ii, which is minor in a major key. In the minor mode the quality of the chord built on 4̂ is minor, so the Roman numeral is also lower case: iv, instead of IV. The ii chord in minor keys is diminished, which is signified by a lower case Roman numeral and a degree sign, as in ii°. Because of the diminished fifth between the root and fifth of the chord, the ii° chord is employed in first inversion exclusively in this module, meaning that 4̂ will be in the bass. Example 2.2 shows these chords as they appear in C major and minor.

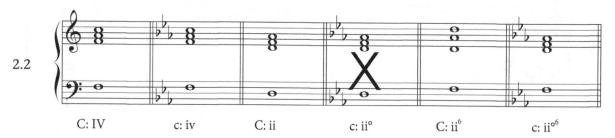

2.2

Examples for Performance

Allegretto

Clayson

2.3

The day-dream is break-ing, The world is a - wak-ing, The

clouds of night's dark - ness are flee - ing a - way.

Deliberatamente

2.4

f

Dictation Practice

2.5

Bb: I

2.6

Eb: I

2.7

Bb: I

2.8

D: IV

2.9

G: I

2.10

Bb: IV

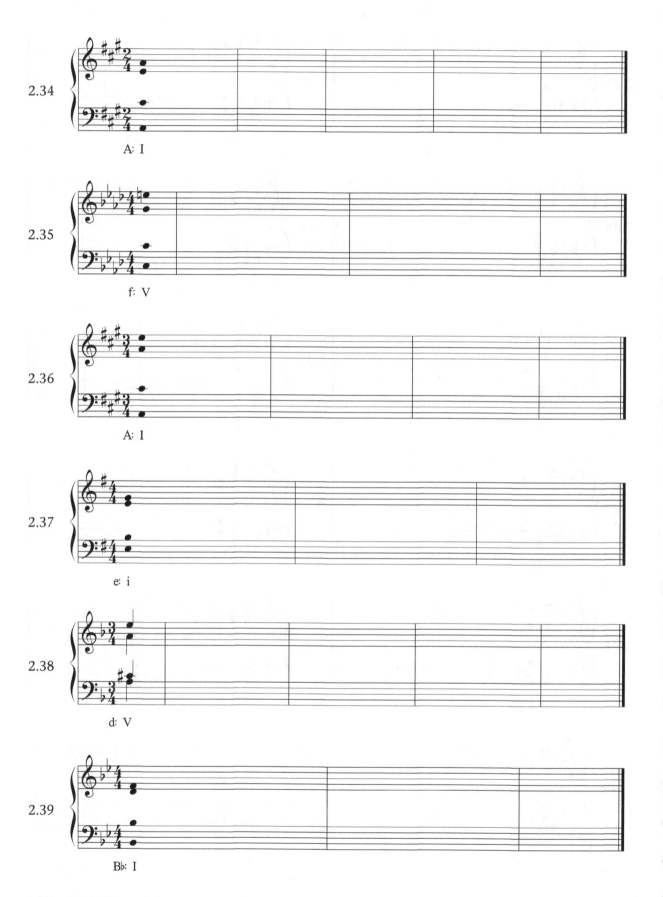

2.34

A: I

2.35

f: V

2.36

A: I

2.37

e: i

2.38

d: V

2.39

B♭: I

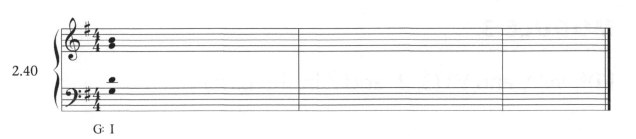

2.40

G: I

MODULE 3

I(i)⁶, vii°⁶, and V⁶ ($\hat{3}$, $\hat{2}$, and $\hat{7}$ in the Bass)

In previous modules the root of each triad was almost always in the bass. The I chord had $\hat{1}$ in the bass, the V chord had $\hat{5}$ in the bass, and so on. The only exception so far is ii⁶, in which the root is $\hat{2}$, but $\hat{4}$ (the third of the chord) is in the bass. Beginning with this module three more chords will be used with a chord member other than the root in the bass: I, V, and vii°. When the root of the chord is in the bass, the chord is said to be in root position, but when the third is in the bass it is in first inversion.

In Example 3.1, the first measure contains three different voicings of the tonic triad, all with E in the bass and therefore all in first inversion. Notice that I and I⁶ support the same scale degrees: $\hat{1}$, $\hat{3}$, and $\hat{5}$, the three members of the tonic triad.

The second measure of Example 3.1 contains two voicings of V⁶. Note that $\hat{7}$ in the bass will not be used to support $\hat{7}$ in the soprano. This is because of the voice leading rule that prohibits doubling the leading-tone. The majority of chords with $\hat{7}$ in the bass are V⁶ chords.

The third measure of Example 3.1 contains three voicings of vii°⁶, a triad that is built on the leading-tone and is introduced here for the first time. Because of the diminished fifth between the root and fifth of this chord (all other diatonic triads having perfect fifths), this chord is used almost exclusively in first inversion.

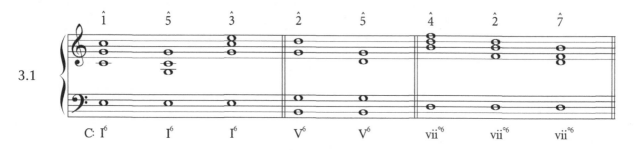

Since vii°⁶ supports many of the same scale degrees as ii and V, it can be tricky to identify. Even so, the diminished fifth mentioned above is so distinctive that, with careful attention and practice, you will acquire the sound of this chord in time. In fact, it is crucial at this point that you begin to pay attention to chord quality. Notice that in each of the first three measures in Example 3.2, three different chord qualities (diminished, minor, and major triads) are used to support the same note in the soprano.

The last measure of Example 3.2 shows a common voice leading pattern that is possible when vii°⁶ comes between I and I6. The points of the "X" connect chord members that are traded between the alto and bass voices as they step in contrary motion. This voice leading nicety is known as a *voice exchange* and is one that you should listen for in this module.

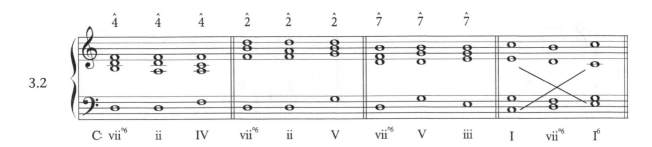

3.2

Example for Performance

3.3

Dictation Practice

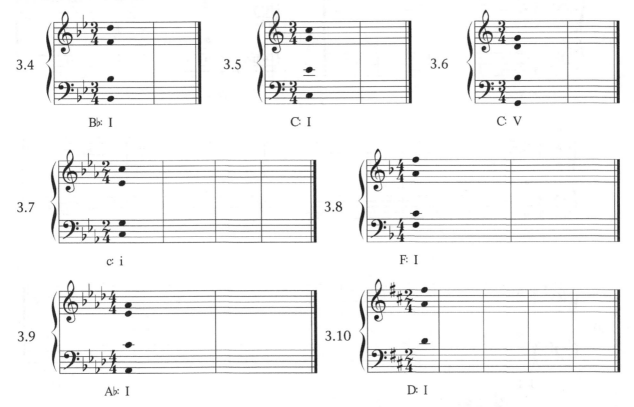

3.4 Bb: I

3.5 C: I

3.6 C: V

3.7 c: i

3.8 F: I

3.9 Ab: I

3.10 D: I

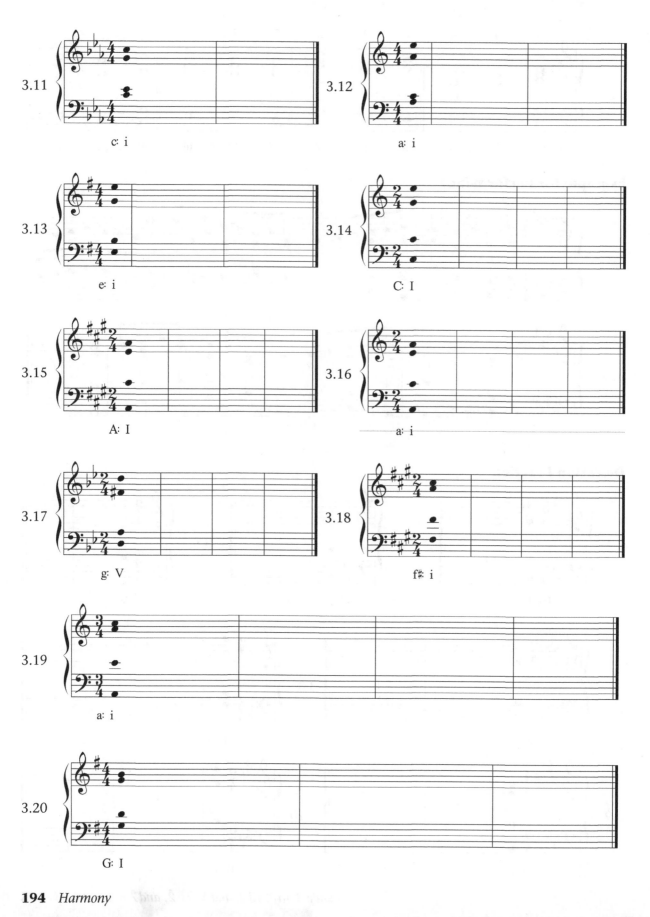

3.11   c: i

3.12   a: i

3.13   e: i

3.14   C: I

3.15   A: I

3.16   a: i

3.17   g: V

3.18   f#: i

3.19   a: i

3.20   G: I

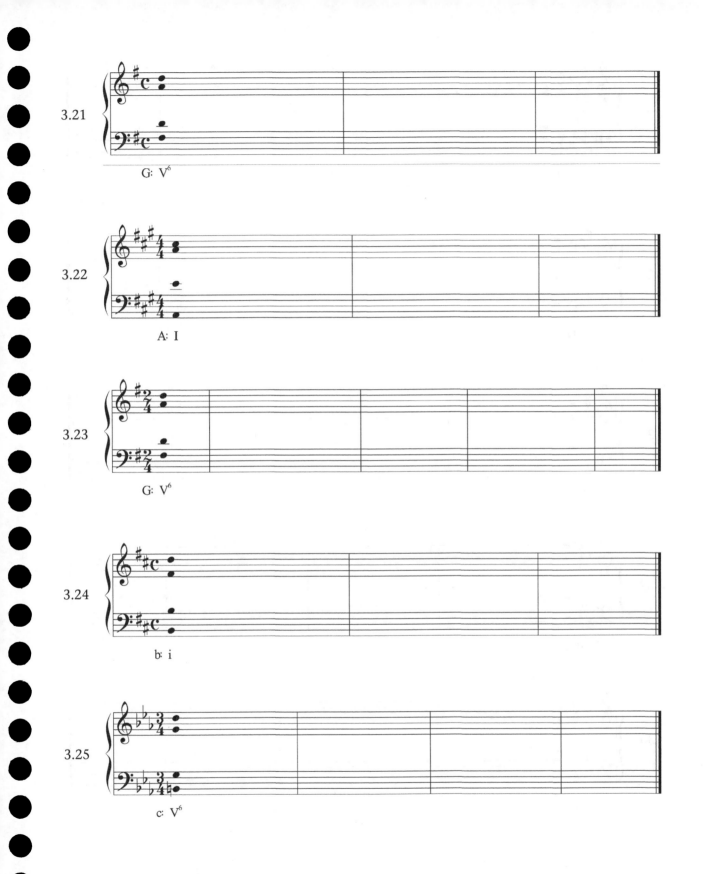

3.21

G: V⁶

3.22

A: I

3.23

G: V⁶

3.24

b: i

3.25

c: V⁶

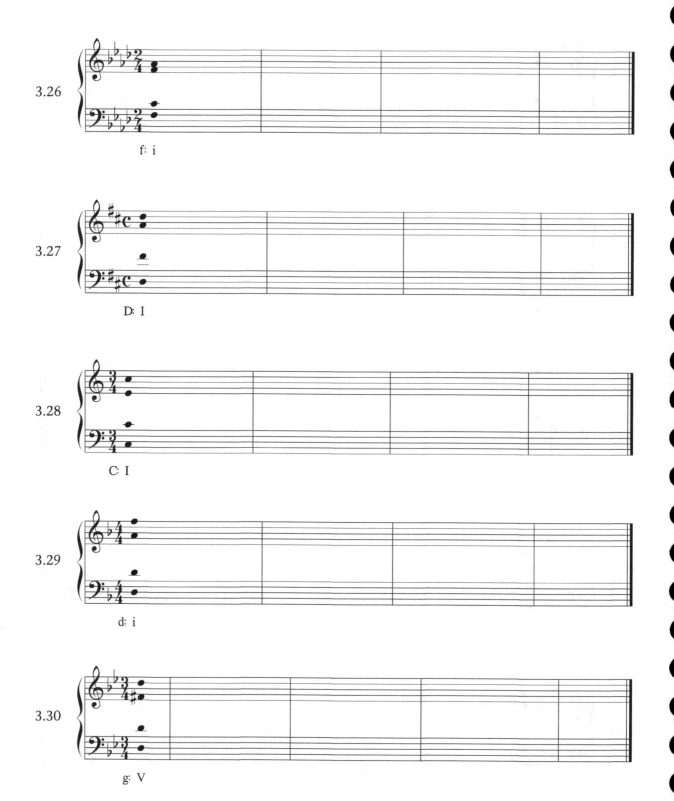

3.31

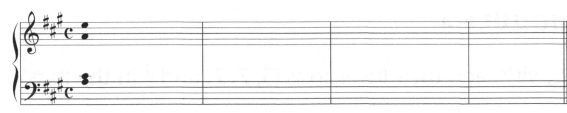

A: I

MODULE 4

V⁷, vii°⁷, and their Inversions (5̂, 7̂, 2̂, and 4̂ in the Bass)

In this module the focus returns to the dominant function as we expand its meaning and potential. While the triad has been the foundation of your study because of its stability, it occasionally becomes necessary to destabilize the triad, to render it more dissonant, and the primary means of accomplishing this is by adding a fourth note, a chordal seventh. Remember that the third of the chord is so named because it is a third above the root, so a seventh similarly is a seventh above the root (not to be confused with 7̂, the leading tone). The dominant seventh, V⁷, is the most common of the diatonic seventh chords by far. Example 4.1 shows three different voicings of V⁷ going to I, followed by the three inversions of V⁷, again resolving to I.

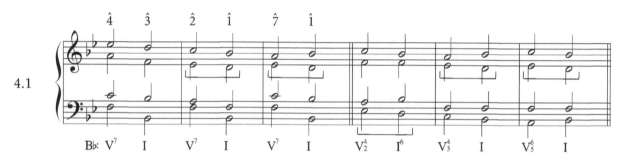

Example 4.1 begins with the seventh of the V⁷ (4̂) resolving to the third of I (3̂) in the soprano. This is an essential voice leading connection and each subsequent resolution uses brackets to show in which voice the 4̂–3̂ resolution occurs. Even if it is in an inner voice, that particular voice leading remains special and will help you hear the difference between V and V⁷.

In addition to V⁷, this module also introduces vii°⁷, which is only available in the minor mode because the root of the chord is the leading-tone and the seventh is ♭6̂. This chord (and each of its inversions) is paired with V⁷ in this module because it shares many of the same essential voice leadings and also typically resolves to i. Example 4.2 shows those voice leadings, including 4̂–3̂, mentioned above, and 6̂–5̂, which is unique to the resolution of vii°⁷ to i.

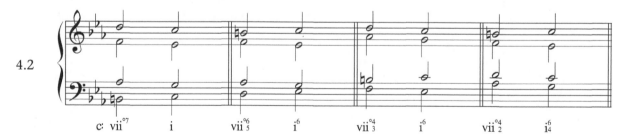

Examples for Performance

4.3 — Allegro maestoso — Mozart

Es le - be Sa - rast - ro! Sa - rast - ro soll le - ben!

Er ist es, dem wir uns mit Freud - en er - ge - ben!

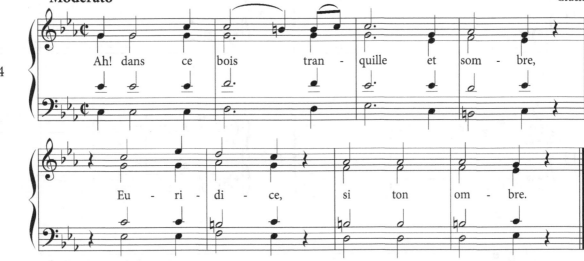

4.4 — Moderato — Gluck

Ah! dans ce bois tran - quille et som - bre,

Eu - ri - di - ce, si ton om - bre.

Dictation Practice

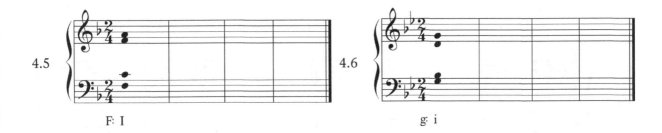

4.5 — F: I

4.6 — g: i

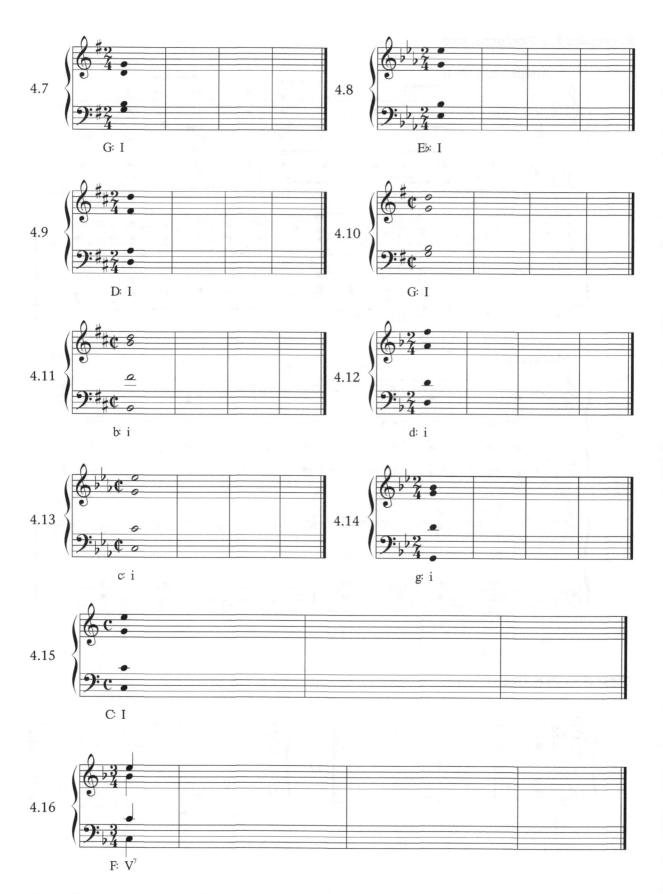

4.17 Bb: I

4.18 G: I

4.19 c: i

4.20 g: i

4.21 e: V

4.22   f: i

4.23   c: i

4.24   B♭: I

4.25   D: I

4.26   G: I

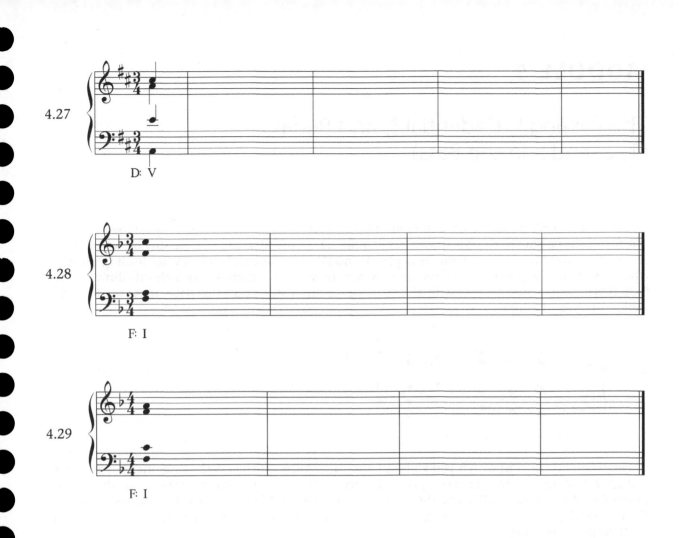

4.27

D: V

4.28

F: I

4.29

F: I

MODULE 5

The Passing $^6_4$, Cadential $^6_4$, and Pedal $^6_4$ ($\hat{1}$, $\hat{2}$, and $\hat{5}$ in the Bass)

The second-inversion triad is less common but predictably occurs in three strictly defined contexts. The first is the passing $^6_4$, which is shown in Example 5.1. In the first case a $^6_4$ is passing between I and I^6 and in the second case a I$^6_4$ is passing between IV and IV^6. The *voice exchange*, a voice leading nicely in which two voices step in contrary motion between the same two members of a chord (shown by the "X") is typical in a passing $^6_4$. As with all the voice leading patterns on this page, these work equally well in major and minor.

5.1

Ab: I   V$^6_4$ I^6 IV   I$^6_4$ IV^6

The second context in which you will find a second-inversion triad is the cadential $^6_4$, which is an embellishment of V at the cadence. A typical voice leading for this $^6_4$ chord is shown in the second-to-last bar of Example 5.2. Because the analysis of this chord differs so much from school to school the cadential $^6_4$ will be analyzed using figured bass but without a Roman numeral. Ask your teacher for their preferred label.

5.2

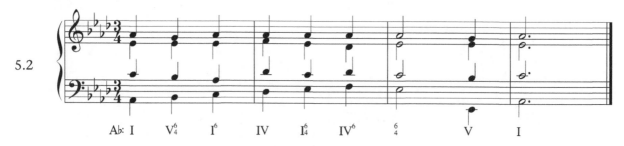

Ab: I   V$^6_4$ I^6 IV   I$^6_4$ IV^6 $^6_4$ V   I

The third context is known as the pedal $^6_4$ (sometimes called a neighbor $^6_4$). The pedal $^6_4$ occurs between the same inversion of the same chord, usually a root-position triad. Example 5.3 builds on Examples 5.1 and 5.2 by ending with a pedal $^6_4$ after the cadence.

5.3

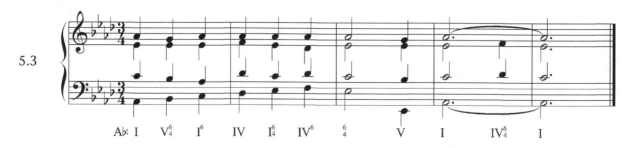

Ab: I   V$^6_4$ I^6 IV   I$^6_4$ IV^6 $^6_4$ V   I   IV$^6_4$ I

Examples for Performance

Parsons

5.4

5.5

Baird

Dictation Practice

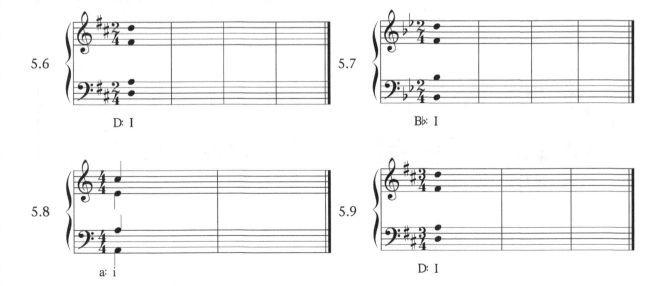

5.6

D: I

5.7

Bb: I

5.8

a: i

5.9

D: I

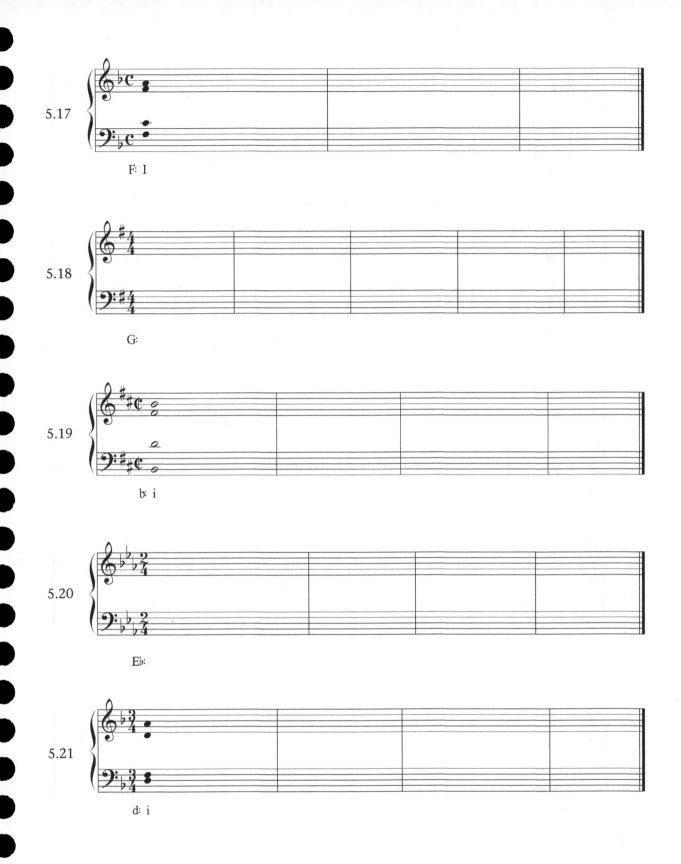

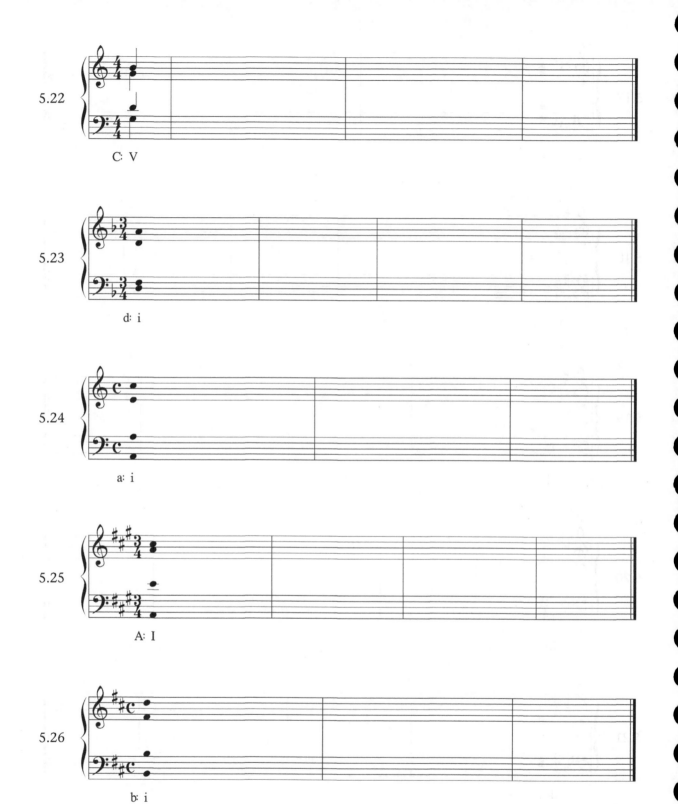

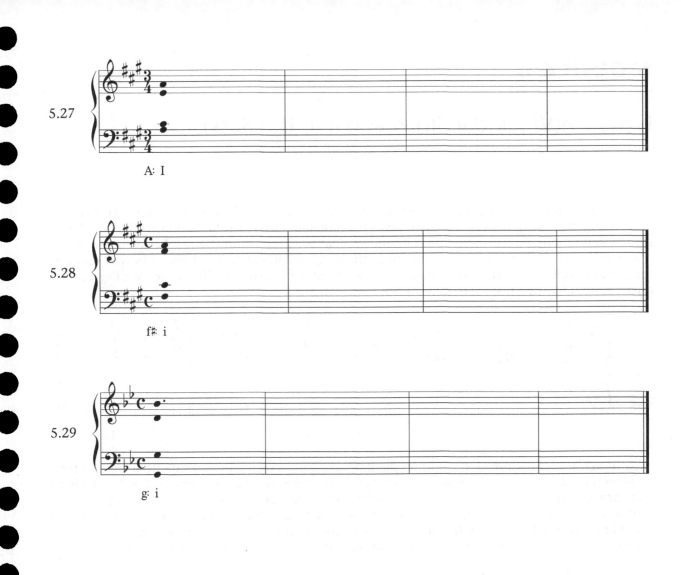

5.27

A: I

5.28

f♯: i

5.29

g: i

MODULE 6

IV(iv)⁶, vi(VI), and iii(III) ($\hat{6}$ and $\hat{3}$ in the Bass)

This chapter introduces the last two stable diatonic triads. The submediant triad, vi, supports $\hat{6}$, $\hat{1}$, and $\hat{3}$, all of which are also supported by harmonies that are more fundamental, reflecting the fact that vi is sometimes thought of as a "bridging" harmony. That is, vi is a chord that lies between harmonies that can be perceived as being more integral to the progression. Example 6.1 shows how vi supports some of the same scale degrees as harmonies you are already familiar with. The same scale degrees and qualities hold for the VI chord in minor keys.

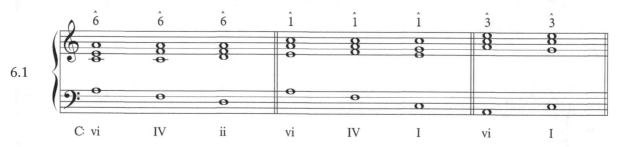

Although it is easily the least common diatonic triad, iii nevertheless appears from time to time and you should be aware of it. Example 6.2 shows the scale degrees that are supported by the iii chord and partially explains why it is so rare. The scale degrees supportable by iii are already strongly associated with I, V, or both. Being that I and V are far more stable and common, it stands to reason that iii should be little used. Note also that iii, when it does appear, most commonly supports $\hat{7}$, as shown in the second measure of this example, and the other two voicings of iii are vanishingly rare.

One peculiarity pertaining to the III chord in minor keys is that it frequently supports the lowered seventh scale degree, $\flat\hat{7}$. A raised leading tone makes the quality of the III chord augmented (see Example 6.3), but augmented triads are even more rare than III chords. Therefore, remember *not* to raise the leading tone if you hear a III chord in minor. Finally, in a minor key the III chord is the tonic of the relative major. In later chapters we will explore this relationship more extensively.

6.3

c: III⁺ III

In addition, this chapter introduces the IV/iv⁶ chord. Example 6.4 shows the scale degrees that are held in common between this chord and the submediant. You will need to pay careful attention to the quality of these chords in order to identify them accurately.

6.4

C: IV⁶   vi   c: iv⁶   VI

Examples for Performance

Andante con moto

6.5

6.6

J. S. Bach

Dictation Practice

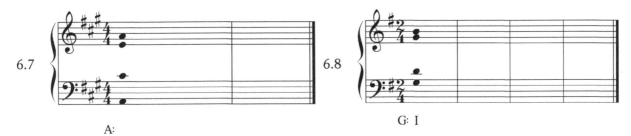

6.7   6.8

A: G: I

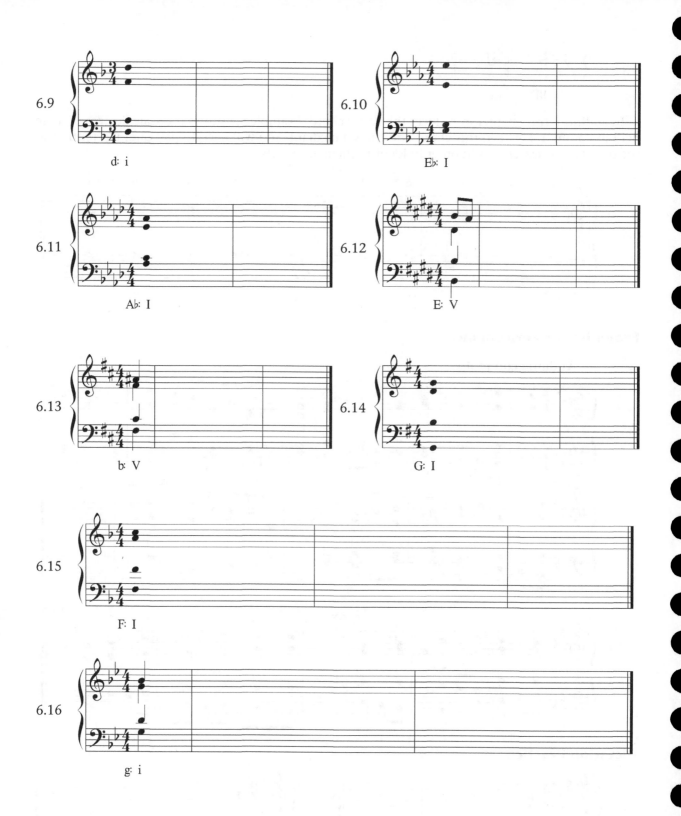

6.9 d: i

6.10 Eb: I

6.11 Ab: I

6.12 E: V

6.13 b: V

6.14 G: I

6.15 F: I

6.16 g: i

6.17   Bb: I

6.18   D: I

6.19   F: I

6.20   c:

6.21   F: I

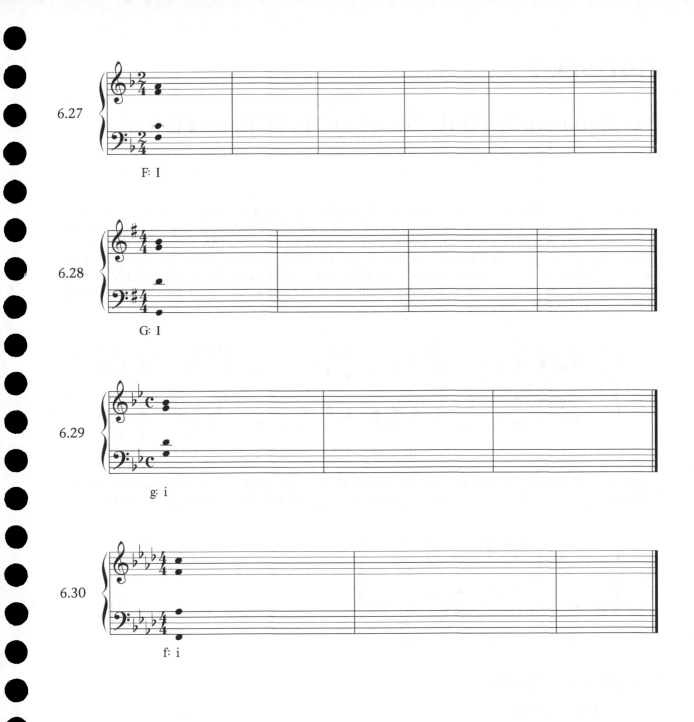

6.27   F: I

6.28   G: I

6.29   g: i

6.30   f: i

MODULE 7

Pre-dominant Seventh Chords: ii($^{(\emptyset)7}$, ii($^{(\emptyset)}$)$^6_5$, and IV(iv)^7

The scale degrees of the supertonic triad are $\hat{2}$, $\hat{4}$, and $\hat{6}$. Scale degrees $\hat{2}$ and $\hat{4}$ have both dominant and pre-dominant associations as they are part of both ii and V^7, while $\hat{6}$ is more securely associated with pre-dominant function. The seventh of a ii^7 is $\hat{1}$, and because it is the seventh of the chord it is dissonant and must resolve down by step. So listen for the downward resolution of $\hat{1}$ to $\hat{7}$. This is true in both the major mode and in minor, where the quality of the supertonic seventh chord is half-diminished (ii$^{\emptyset7}$). As with ii°, ii$^{\emptyset7}$ is commonly heard in first inversion. Example 7.1 shows three typical voice leadings for this chord.

7.1

Just as the ii^7 chord destabilizes $\hat{1}$, the IV^7 chord destabilizes $\hat{3}$, an otherwise stable scale degree. Unlike ii^7, IV^7 almost always appears in root position. A typical voice leading is shown in Example 7.2.

7.2

Examples for Performance

7.3

7.3

Ma - ri - a aus-er - ko - ren ein Kind-lein hat ge - bo - ren zu

Beth-lem in dem Stall, _____ zu Beth-lem in dem Stall.

Palmer

7.4

Dictation Practice

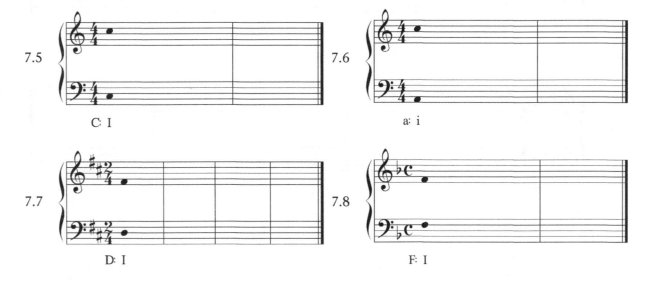

7.5

C: I

7.6

a: i

7.7

D: I

7.8

F: I

7.17

G: I

7.18

d: i

7.19

G: V⁷

7.20

A: I

7.21

A♭: I

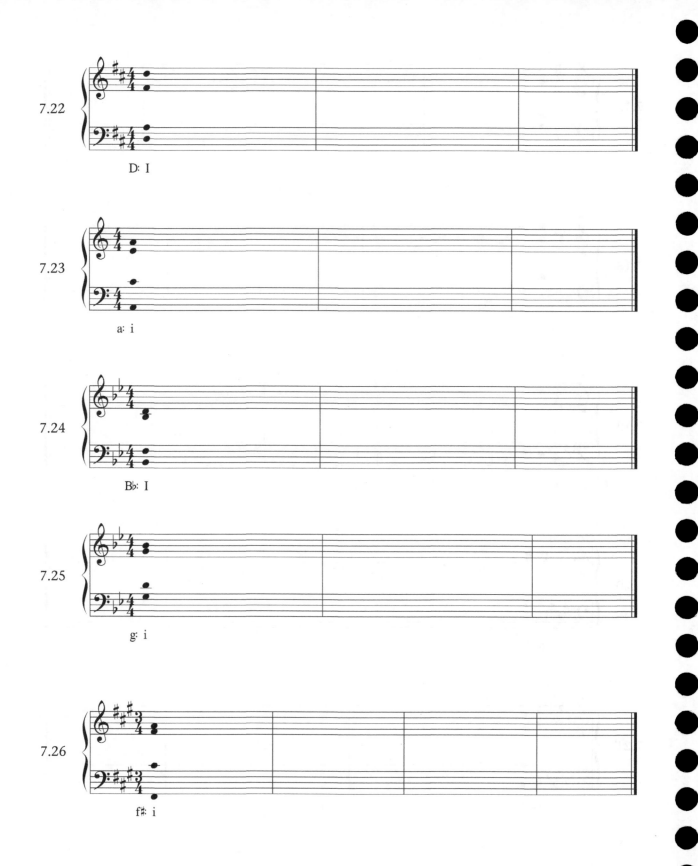

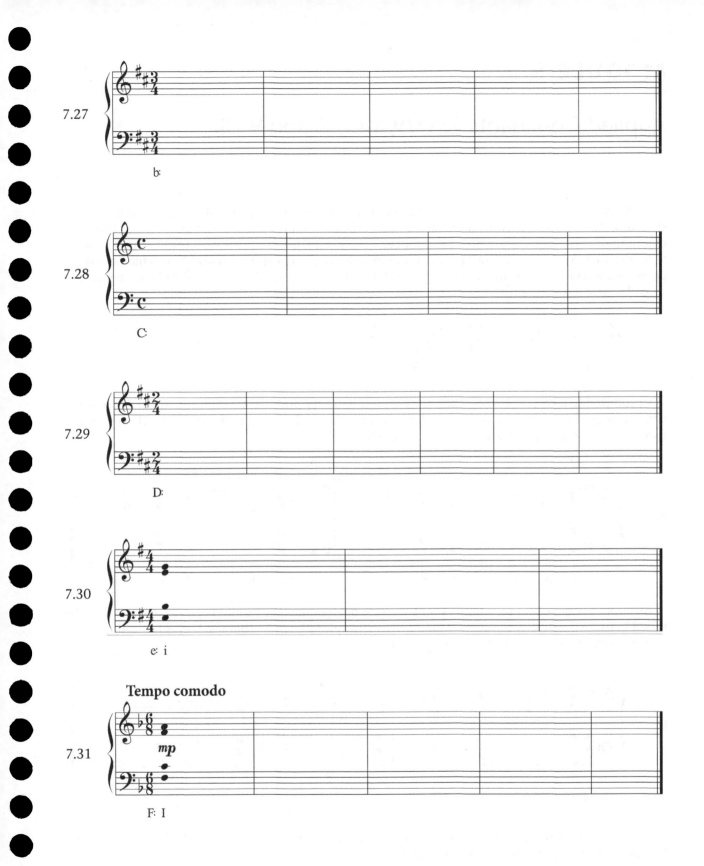

7.27

b:

7.28

C:

7.29

D:

7.30

e: i

Tempo comodo

7.31

mp

F: I

MODULE 8

Applied Dominants 1: V⁷/V, vii°⁷/V, and V⁷/III

This chapter is the first of several that will focus on harmonies that include notes outside the key signature. Such harmonies are known as *chromatic* harmonies (as opposed to diatonic), and the most common of them by far is the V/V (pronounced "five of five"). A simple way to think of this chord is as a chromatic variety of ii. Example 8.1 presents a direct comparison of ii and V/V, which are composed of the exact same scale degrees. The only difference between them is the ♯$\hat{4}$ in V/V. The same is true of ii⁷ and V⁷/V.

8.1

In addition to having every scale degree in common, both ii and V/V are typically (if not exclusively) employed as chords that proceed convincingly to V. Example 8.2 has the same chord progression twice, with V/V taking the place of ii the second time.

8.2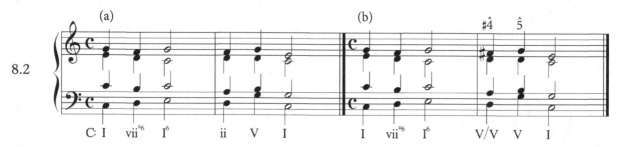

Example 8.3 shows that in minor keys two scale degrees have to be altered; $\hat{4}$ and $\hat{6}$ must both be raised to make the quality of the triad major. This example also shows that the ♯$\hat{4}$–$\hat{5}$ voice leading must be maintained even when the V⁷/V is inverted.

8.3

Example 8.4 shows typical voice leading for vii°⁷/V, which is characterized by ♯$\hat{4}$–$\hat{5}$ and ♭$\hat{3}$–2 (in the bass and tenor, respectively, in this example).

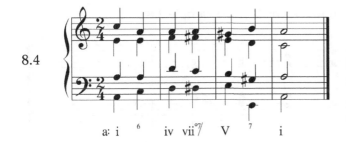

8.4

a: i   6   iv   vii°⁷/   V   7   i

The other voice leading that is typically maintained is Î–$\hat{7}$ in V⁷/V–I because Î is the chordal seventh of the V⁷/V and must resolve down by step. This is identical in resolution to the seventh when ii⁷ goes to V.

In the minor mode it is also very common to tonicize the mediant, III. This harmonic motion sounds very natural to us because III is the tonal center of the relative major. Example 8.5 presents a harmonic pattern that features V/III and is known as *la folia*. In m. 1 C♯ acts as a leading-tone in dominant harmony, but in m. 2 C♯ acts as the root of a dominant that points to III, as if the middle three chords were really in F major.

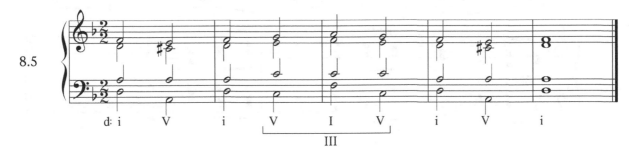

8.5

d: i   V   i   V   I   V   i   V   i

III

It is a simple thing to modify this basic pattern in order to match later styles. Example 8.6 begins like a *folia*, then cadences in a more modern style.

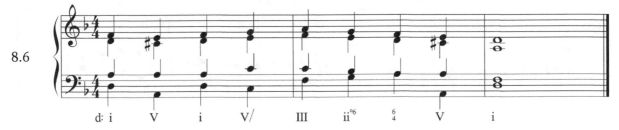

8.6

d: i   V   i   V/   III   ii°⁶   6/4   V   i

The addition of a diatonic seventh on the V/III results in a dominant seventh (a major triad with a minor seventh) and an even stronger pull to III, as you might be able to hear in Example 8.7.

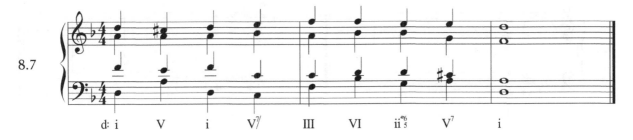

8.7

d: i   V   i   V⁷/   III   VI   ii°⁶₅   V⁷   i

Finally, as with all applied chords, it is possible to invert the V⁷/III (Example 8.8).

8.8

d: i   iv   i   V$^6_5$/   III   iv⁷ $^6_4$ V⁷   i

Examples for Performance

Mason

8.9

Schütz

8.10

My soul now mag - ni - fies__ the Lord; My spir - it leaps for joy__ in him.

Dictation Practice

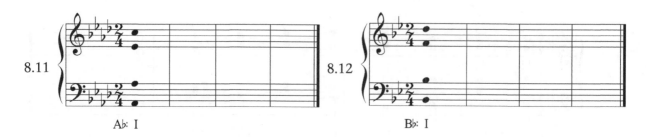

8.11   A♭: I   8.12   B♭: I

8.22

Bb: I

8.23

d: i

8.24

C:

8.25

Bb: I

8.26

d: i

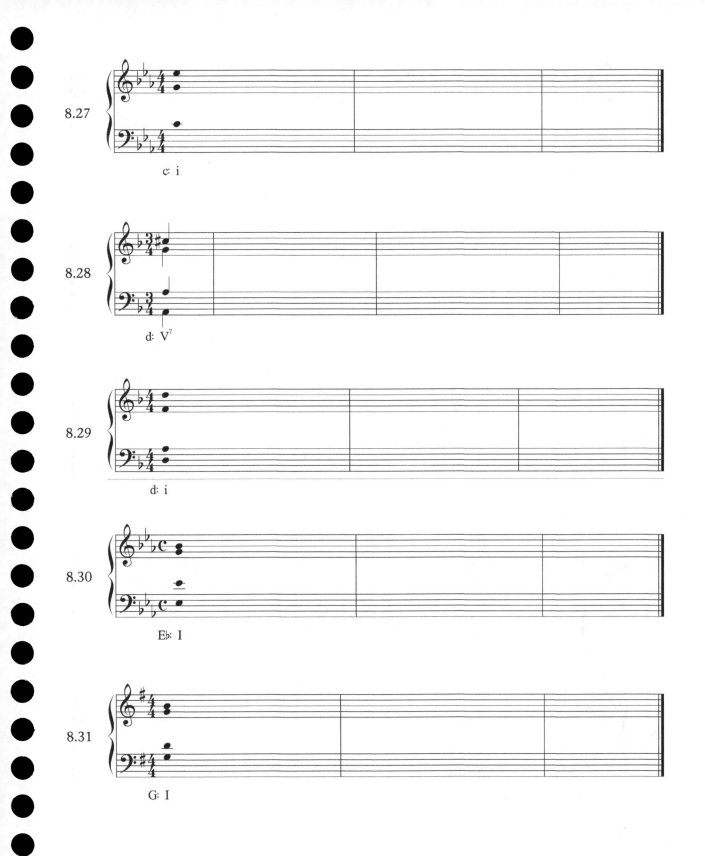

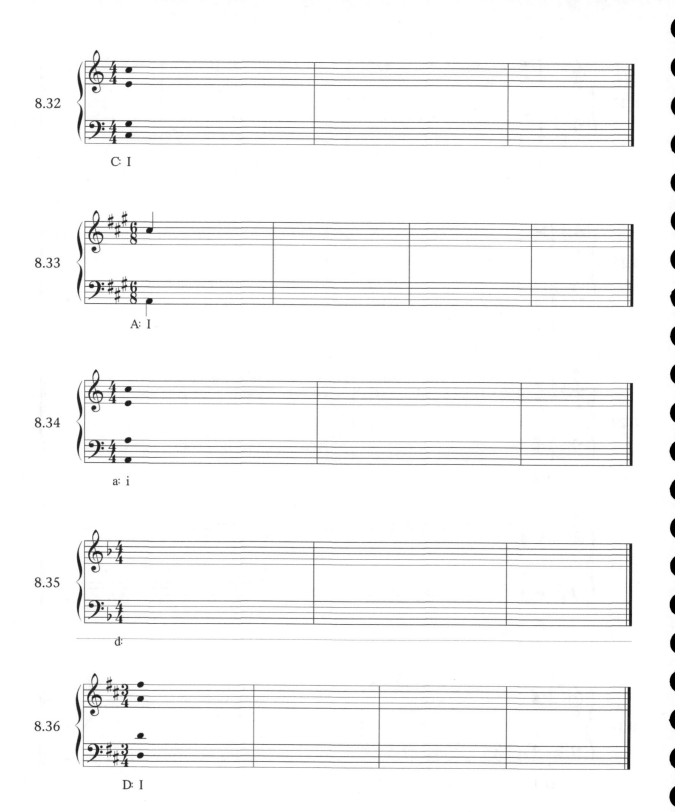

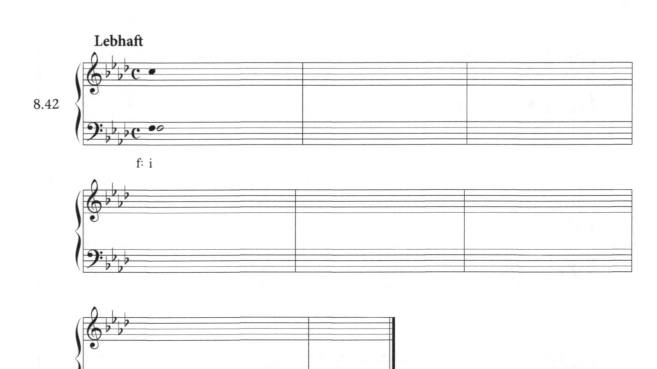

f: i

MODULE 9

Applied Dominants 2: V⁷/IV(iv) and vii°⁷/iv

Just as the resolution of V⁷/V to V had a characteristic, though temporary leading-tone in the resolution of #4̂ to 5̂, every other applied chord has its own unique leading-tone resolution. In V⁷/IV the characteristic leading-tone is raised 3̂, which is diatonic in major keys and chromatic in minor keys. Conversely, the temporary subdominant is ♭7̂, which is chromatic in major keys, but diatonic in minor keys. Example 9.1 shows this chord first in a major key and then in its parallel minor.

9.1

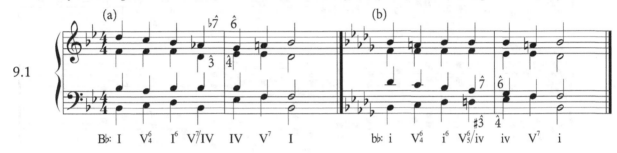

The vii°⁷/iv is built on raised 3̂, which once again acts as the temporary leading-tone, and has ♭2̂ for a seventh (see Example 9.2). This chord will only be used in this module to tonicize iv in minor keys.

9.2

Examples for Performance

J.S. Bach

9.3

J.S. Bach

9.4

Dictation Practice

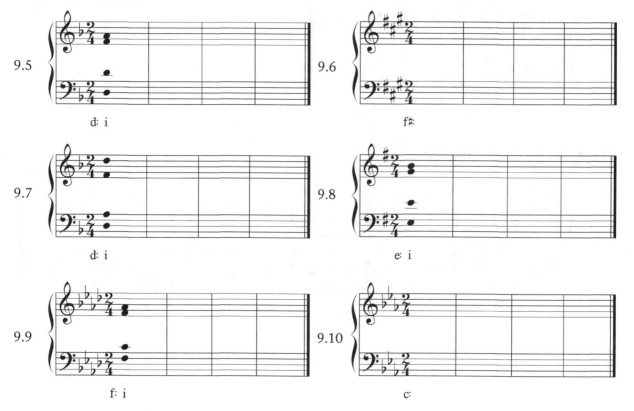

9.5 d: i

9.6 f♯:

9.7 d: i

9.8 e: i

9.9 f: i

9.10 c:

9.17

d: i

9.18

B♭: I

9.19

C: I

9.20

G: I

9.21

D: I

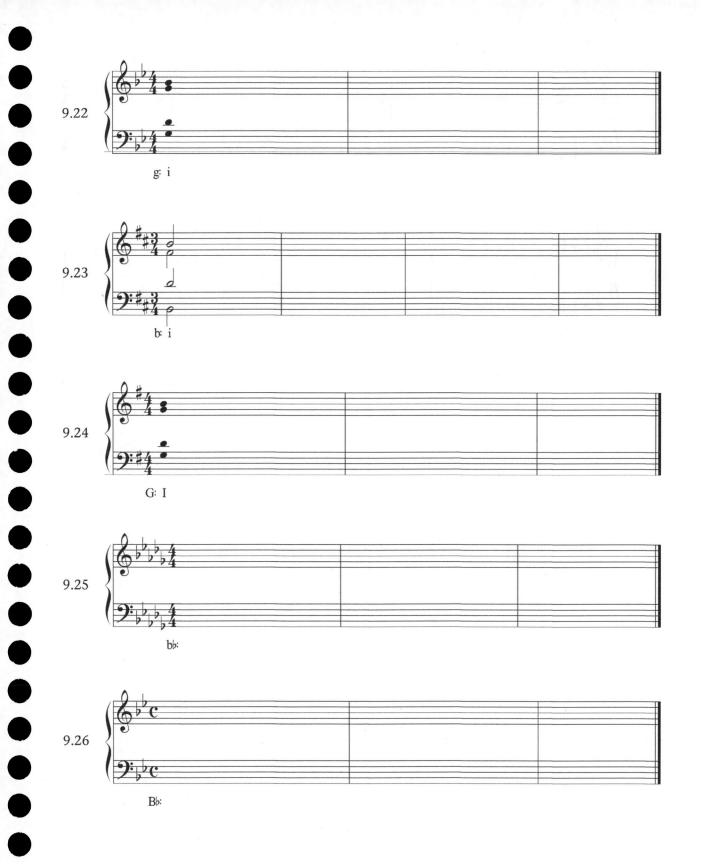

9.22

g: i

9.23

b: i

9.24

G: I

9.25

b♭:

9.26

B♭:

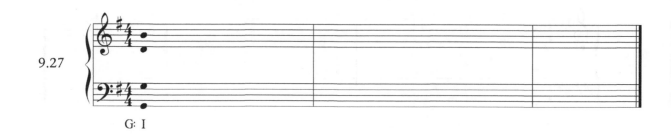

9.27

G: I

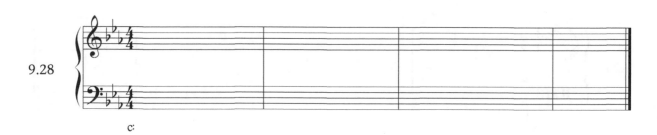

9.28

c:

MODULE 10

Applied Dominants 3: V⁷/ii, vii°⁷/ii, V⁷/vi(VI), and vii°⁷/vi

By now you should be comfortable with the concept and typical voice leading of applied chords, so the following is simply an overview of the particular examples that are the focus of this module.

Example 10.1 shows V⁷ tonicizing ii in a major key. (In minor keys the supertonic triad is diminished, ii°, so it will not be tonicized.) #$\hat{1}$ functions as the temporary leading-tone, while $\hat{5}$ is the chordal seventh and resolves down to $\hat{4}$.

10.1

D: I   V⁷   I   V⁷/ii   ii   V⁷   I

In Example 10.2, V⁷ is applied to both vi in a major key and to VI in its parallel minor.

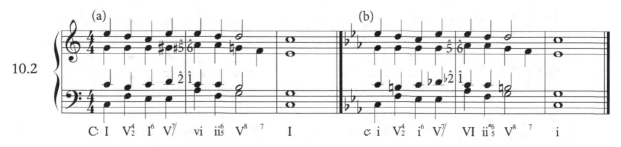

10.2

C: I   V$_2^4$ I⁶   V⁷/   vi   ii$_5^{o6}$ V⁸   ⁷   I

c: i   V$_2^4$ i⁶   V⁷/   VI   ii$_5^{ø6}$ V⁸   ⁷   i

In Examples 10.3 and 10.4, vii°⁷ is used to tonicize ii and vi. Because such examples are vanishingly rare, VI in minor keys will not be tonicized using vii°⁷ in this module.

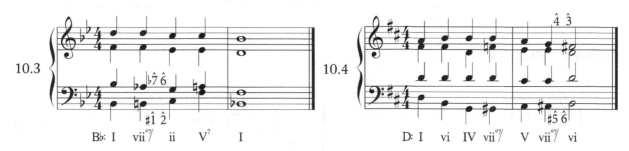

10.3

B♭: I   vii°⁷/   ii   V⁷   I

10.4

D: I   vi   IV   vii°⁷/   V   vii°⁷/   vi

Examples for Performance

10.5

~ Mason

Filitz

10.6

Dictation Practice

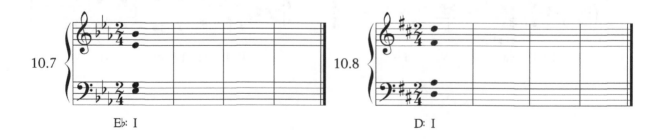

10.7

Eb: I

10.8

D: I

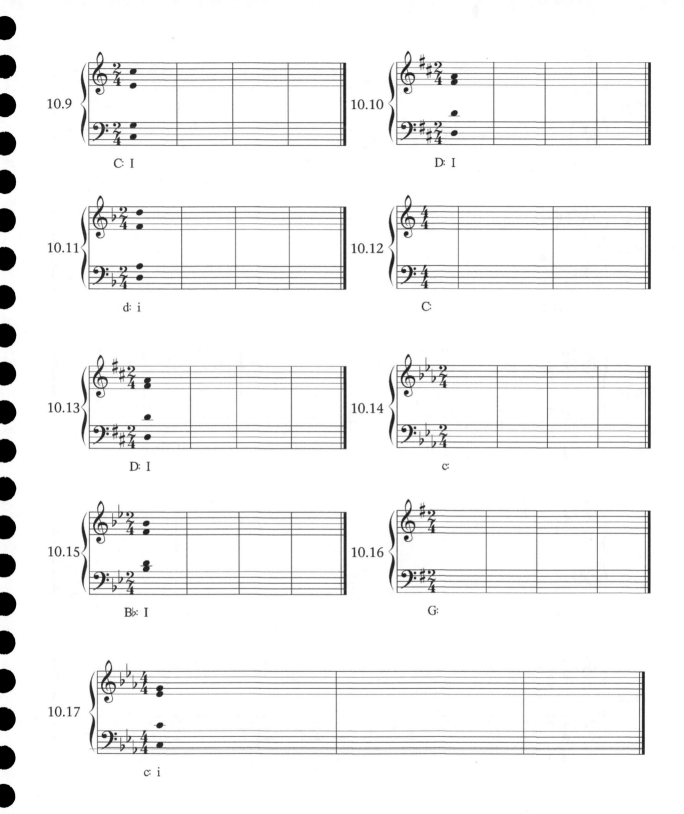

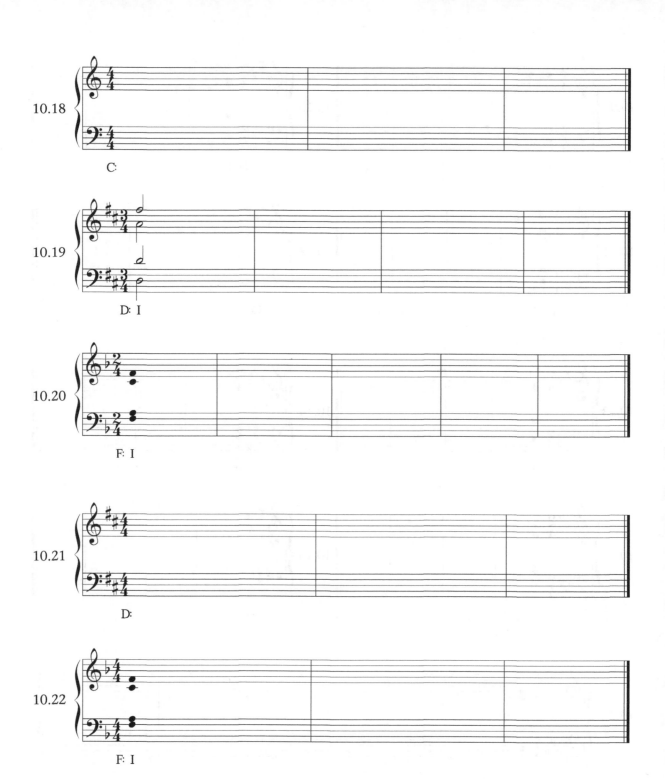

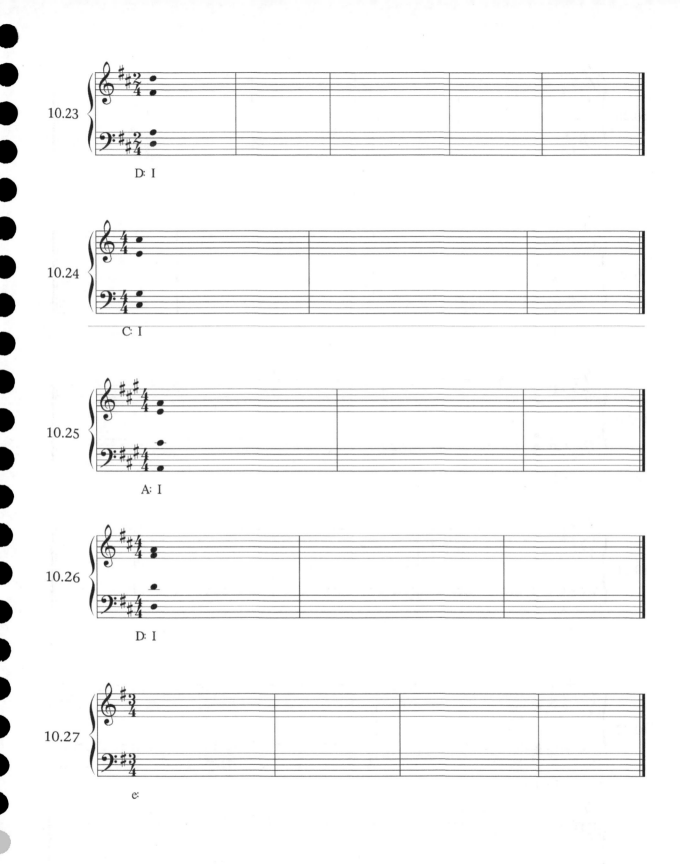

10.23

D: I

10.24

C: I

10.25

A: I

10.26

D: I

10.27

e:

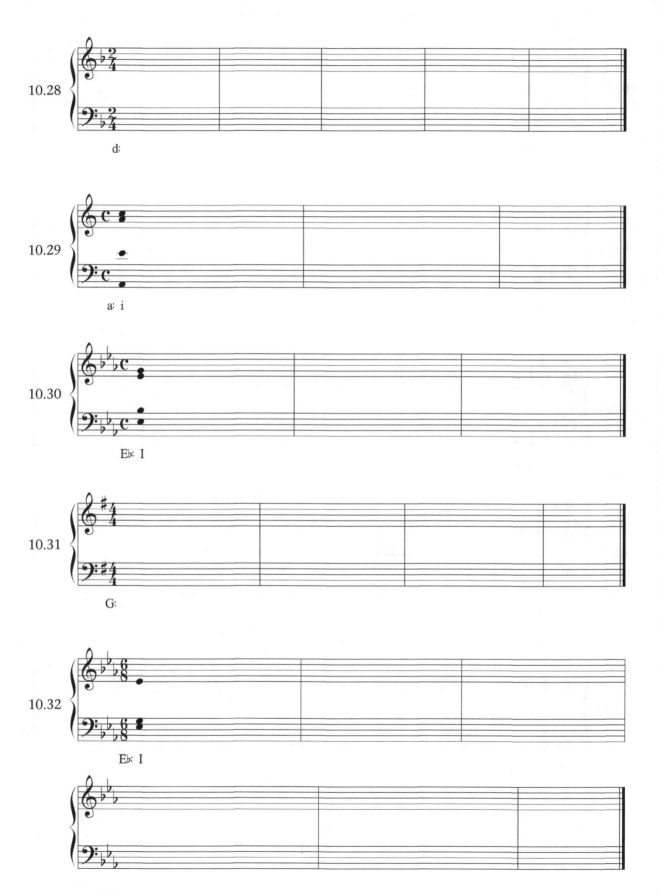

MODULE 11

Modulation to Closely Related Keys

In this module harmonic progressions will shift from one key into another by reinterpreting a single chord that is diatonic in both keys. This process is known as modulation and the common chord is referred to as a diatonic pivot chord.

On the first hearing of the examples in this module you should be transcribing as much as you can in the original key then listening for the beat in which you hear a chromatic shift, which may register as nothing more than a vaguely unexpected harmony. Following that, pay careful attention to the voice leading at the cadence. Even if you don't know what key the example modulated to, you can still write down the kind of cadence you hear (e.g., PAC, IAC, HC, etc.) and the scale degrees you hear in the outer voices.

On subsequent hearings you can begin to fill in details, working forward from the first chords *and* working backward from the end. Your work will eventually meet in the middle, usually right around the moment of modulation. Pay attention to the changing identity of the scale degrees in the outer voices at that point. Example 11.1 shows a typical modulation and points out all of the things mentioned in this paragraph.

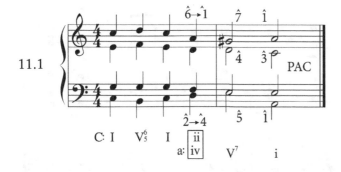

11.1

Closely related keys are those that have either the same key signature or one with only one accidental different from the key signature of origin. For example, if a melody begins in the key of D major, the major keys that are closely related are G and A because the latter has one more sharp and the former one fewer. The minor keys that are closely related to D major are B minor, E minor, and F♯ minor. Example 11.2 shows the segment of the circle of fifths that includes the keys that are closely related to D major. Why is it that C major and A minor are *not* closely related to D major?

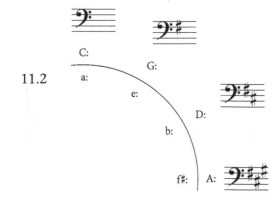

11.2

Notice also that all six of the tonal centers represented by the keys that are closely related to D major are also scale degrees in that key: D, E, F♯, G, A, and B. Furthermore, D major, E minor, F♯ minor, G major, A major, and B minor are all diatonic triads in D major.

Examples for Performance

J. S. Bach

11.3

J. S. Bach

11.4

Dictation Practice

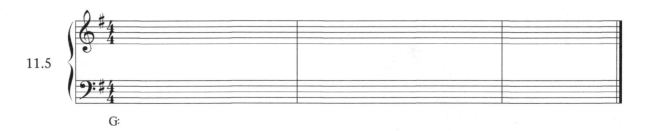

11.5

G:

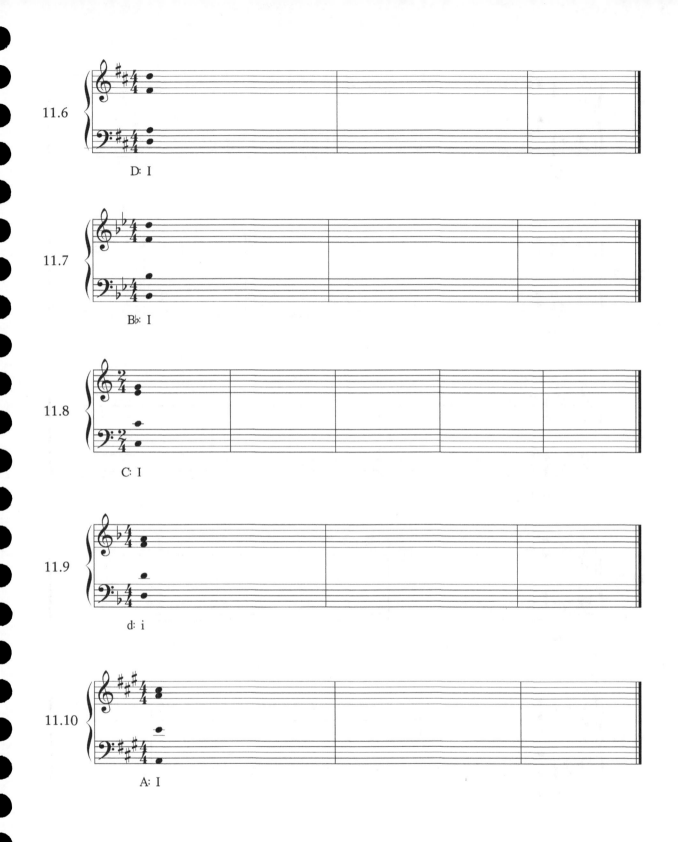

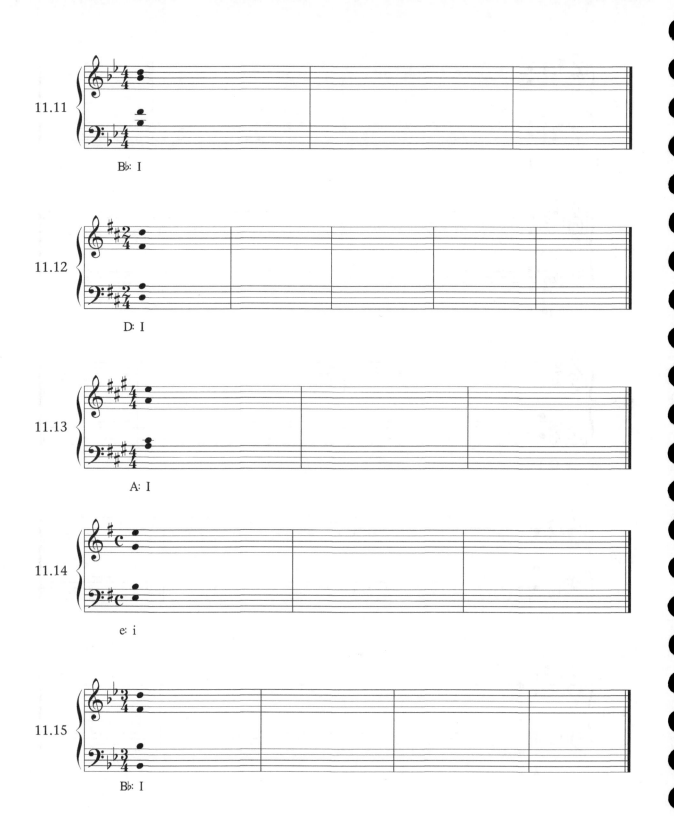

11.16   a: i

11.17   a: i

11.18   D:

11.19   F: I

11.20   F: I

11.21

C: I

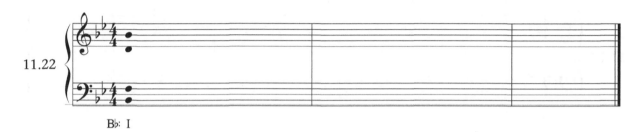

11.22

B♭: I

11.23

C: I

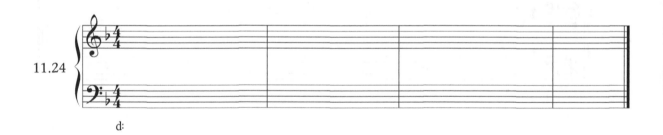

11.24

d:

Adagio

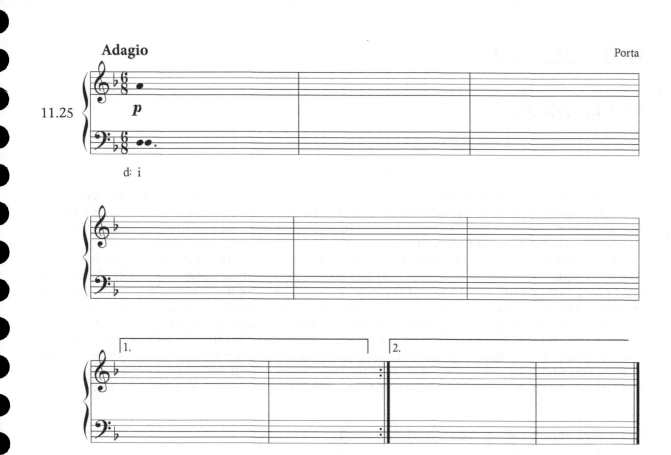

11.25

d: i

MODULE 12

Modal Mixture

Two keys that contrast in mode but share the same tonic (e.g., D major and D minor) are referred to as *parallel* major and minor, and music that freely intermixes the scale degrees of two parallel keys is said to contain *modal mixture*, also known as modal borrowing. Because the tonal center doesn't shift, this is not a modulation but only a change of mode.

The clearest and most characteristic examples of modal mixture take place when the prevailing mode is major and the parallel minor is expressed through relatively brief chromatic alterations. Example 12.1 is primarily in the key of D major, although m. 1, beat 4 includes a B♭, which implies D minor. The voice leading into and out of the B♭ can be thought of as a chromatic neighbor tone in the alto voice that embellishes $\hat{5}$. In another sense, though, it is actually the diatonic $\hat{6}$ in D minor, which turns diatonic IV into iv, suggesting a temporary shift from D major to its parallel, D minor. Notice that the B♭ resolves down by step to $\hat{5}$, just as a tendency tone (even a borrowed one) should. This same pitch, ♭$\hat{6}$ is also the fifth of the two chords, which will be diminished, just as it is diatonically in the minor mode. In either case, listen for the characteristic ♭$\hat{6}$–$\hat{5}$ voice leading.

12.1

Another scale degree that can signal modal mixture is ♭$\hat{3}$, heard on the downbeat of m. 2 in Example 12.2.

12.2

Two more mixture chords will also be featured in this module, ♭VI and ♭III, both of which require two scale degrees to be borrowed from the parallel minor. A triad built on ♭$\hat{6}$ in the major mode would have $\hat{3}$ for a fifth, which is an augmented fifth above ♭$\hat{6}$, so the typical choice is to borrow ♭$\hat{6}$ and ♭$\hat{3}$ in combination, so as to mimic the diatonic VI of the minor mode. The same is true of ♭III, although the fifth of the chord is ♭$\hat{7}$. Both ♭VI and ♭III appear in Example 12.3, as does iv.

C: I   ♭III   IV   V $^4_2$ I^6 I   ♭VI   iv   V^4 3

Finally, in a lament, or step-descent bass, the bass line descends in stepwise motion from $\hat{1}$ to $\hat{5}$ and modal mixture can be used to chromaticize that bass line. Example 12.4 shows just one of many, many possible harmonizations in order to illustrate the point.

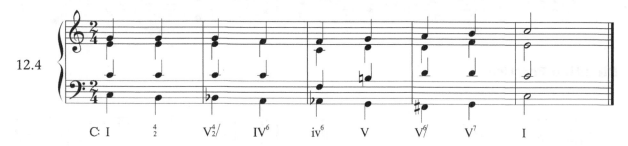

C: I $^4_2$ V$^4_2$/   IV^6 iv^6 V   V^6/   V^7 I

Examples for Performance

Warren

12.6   Beirly

Dictation Practice

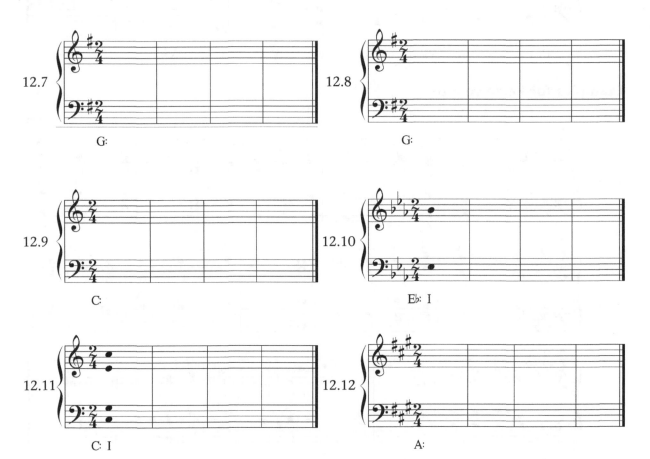

12.7   G:

12.8   G:

12.9   C:

12.10   E♭: I

12.11   C: I

12.12   A:

12.23

G:

12.24

B♭:

12.25

F:

12.26

G:

12.27

mf

G: I

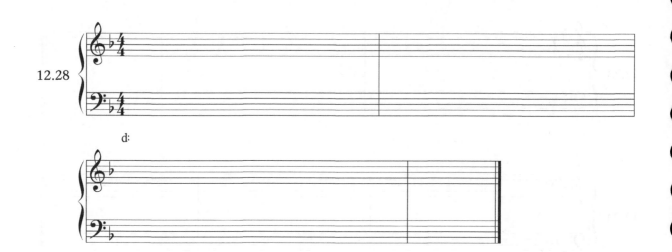

12.28

d:

MODULE 13

The Neapolitan (♭II)

The Neapolitan triad is built on the lowered supertonic, ♭$\hat{2}$, and is a chromatic variant of the ii° chord that is diatonic in the minor mode. It most typically appears in first inversion, with $\hat{4}$ in the bass, although it does occasionally appear in root position. ♭$\hat{2}$ is a tendency tone and usually resolves down to $\hat{7}$, occasionally passing through $\hat{1}$ on the way. In this context $\hat{1}$ is usually harmonized with either a cadential $^6_4$ or vii°⁷/V. Three typical uses of ♭II are shown in Example 13.1.

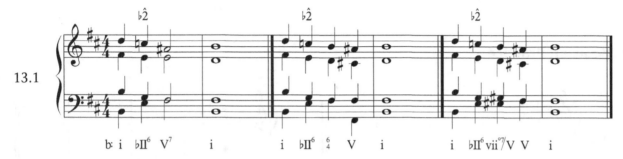

13.1

Examples for Performance

13.2

J. S. Bach

Grave

13.3

Dictation Practice

13.4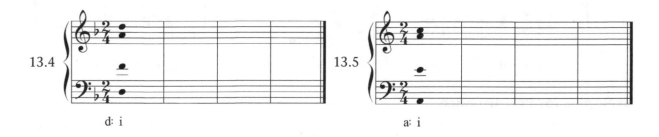

d: i

13.5

a: i

13.6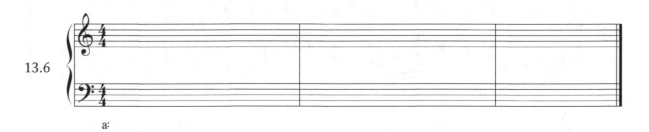

a:

13.7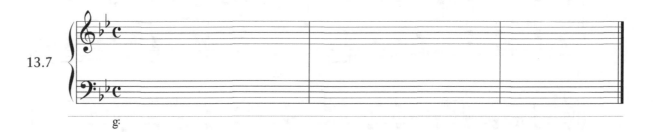

g:

13.13   g: i

13.14   c: V⁷

13.15   A:

13.16   e: i

13.17   a:

13.18

F: I

13.19

b: i

13.20

d:

13.21

D:

13.22

d:

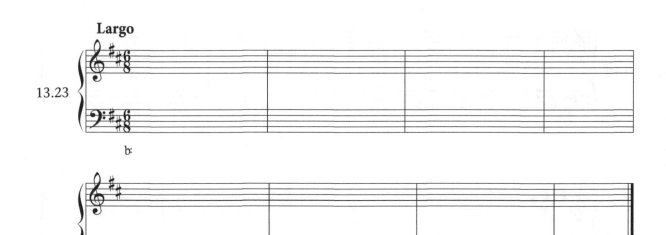

13.23

MODULE 14

Augmented Sixth Chords

The augmented sixth chord is so named because of its characteristic interval: an augmented sixth above the bass. In its most common formulation the augmented sixth chord is built on ♭6̂ in the bass and serves to prepare the dominant. In addition, the augmented sixth interval is filled in with a major third above the bass, which is scale degree 1̂. If only these three scale degrees are present, then the chord is called an Italian sixth. Its resolution is shown in Example 14.1.

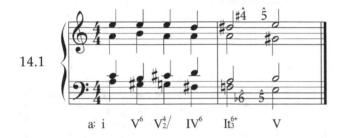

14.1

a: i   V⁶   V⁴₂/   IV⁶   It₃⁶⁺   V

The three most common augmented-sixth chords are the Italian, the French, and the German sixths. In addition to the three tones of the Italian sixth, the French sixth adds scale degree 2̂ and the German sixth adds ♭3̂ (diatonic 3̂ in minor keys). Example 14.2 shows typical resolutions.

14.2

a: Fr₃⁶⁺   V   A: Ger₃⁶⁺   ⁶₄   V

Note: Although the Italian and French sixths *can* go to a cadential ⁶₄ and on to V, the German sixth is the only one that *must* do so in order to avoid parallel fifths with the bass.

Examples for Performance

J. S. Bach

14.3

14.3

Feierlich

Beethoven

14.4

Heil' - ge Nacht, o gie - ße du Him - mels - frie - den in__ dies__ Herz,
bring' dem ar - men Pil - ger Ruh, hol - de La - bung sei - nem Schmerz!

Hell schon er glühn die Ster - ne, grü - ßen aus blau - er Fer - ne:
Glüht nur, ihr hold - nen Ster - ne, wink - end aus blau - er Fer - ne:

Möch - te zu euch so ger - ne fliehn him - mel wärts.
Möch - te zu euch so ger - ne fliehn him - mel wärts.

Maestoso

14.5

Dictation Practice

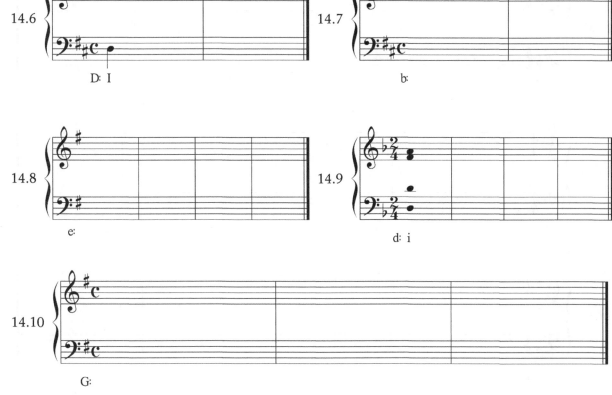

14.6   D: I

14.7   b:

14.8   e:

14.9   d: i

14.10   G:

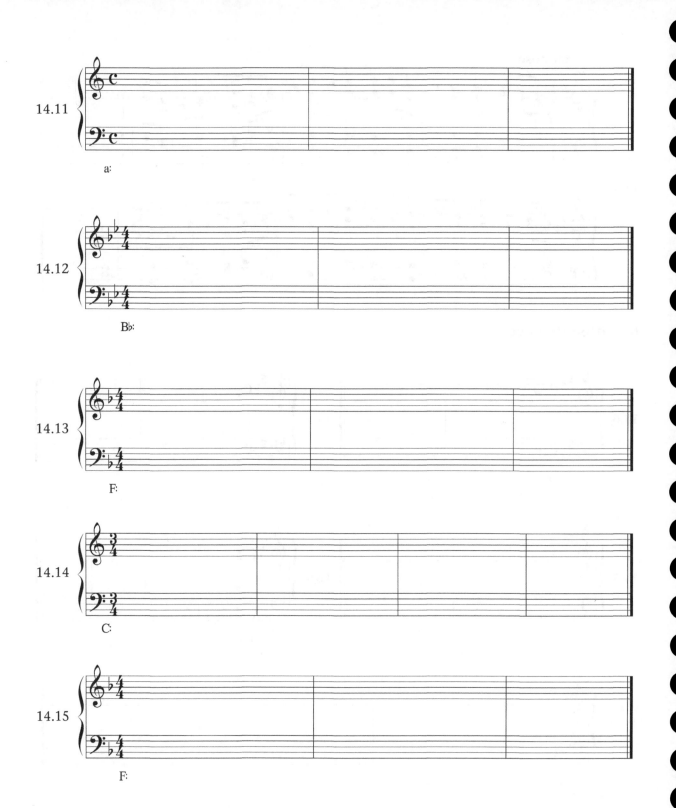

14.11 a:

14.12 B♭:

14.13 F:

14.14 C:

14.15 F:

14.21

F:

14.22

G:

14.23

e: i

14.24

a:

14.25

D: I

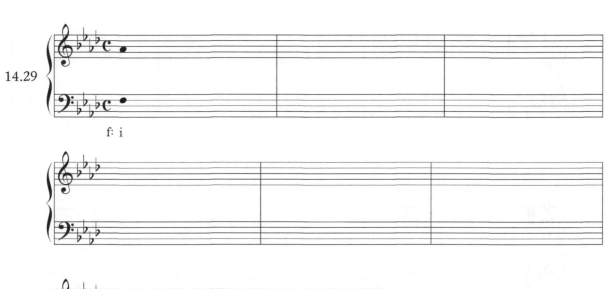

14.29

f: i

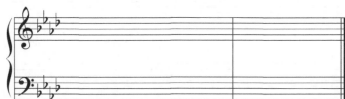

MODULE 15

Modulations Using vii°⁷ and the ct°⁷

Enharmonic Reinterpretation of vii°⁷

The fully diminished seventh chord, vii°⁷, is symmetrical, which is to say that it is constructed entirely of a single interval, the minor 3rd. The interval from the seventh to the root is an augmented 2nd, which is enharmonic to a minor 3rd (see Example 15.1). The property of symmetry renders the °⁷ chord ambiguous in that it is truly impossible to determine the root of this chord by ear. One could never be quite sure whether it was in root position or in one of its inversions.

This property makes the °⁷ chord ideal for modulation because it can resolve in four different directions. Example 15.2 illustrates how a vii°⁶₅ in A minor can resolve as vii°⁷ in C minor. Pay special attention to the tenor line, in which the seventh of the chord is spelled as A♭, the seventh of the chord in C minor, but is understood as also being G♯, the root of the chord in A minor.

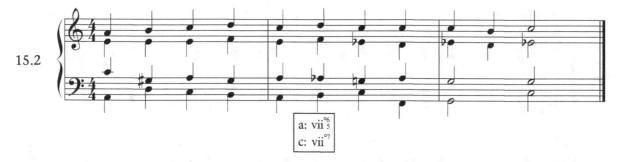

Keep in mind as you work through this module that modal mixture makes vii°⁷ available in major keys and that vii°⁷ can be applied to chords other than i.

The Common-tone °⁷

The common-tone °⁷ (ct°⁷) is a non-functional embellishing chord in which every note of the chord except for the root is a neighbor tone to the chord before and after it. The root of the chord is held in common with the chord being embellished; hence the name of the chord. Example 15.3a shows how a ct°⁷ embellishes an F-major triad. Keep in mind the fact that this major triad can be any function: I in the key of F, IV in C, VI in A minor, and so on. Example 15.3b puts that same voice leading in a harmonic context.

15.3

C: I   V$_3^4$ I^6 IV   ct^{o7} IV $^6_4$ V^7 I

Examples for Performance

Maker

15.4

Moderato

von Weber

15.5

Dictation Practice

15.6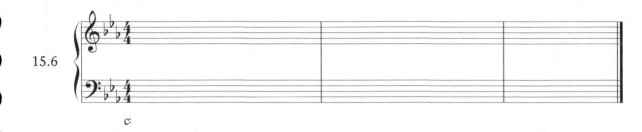

c:

15.7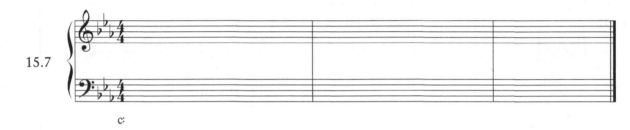

c:

15.8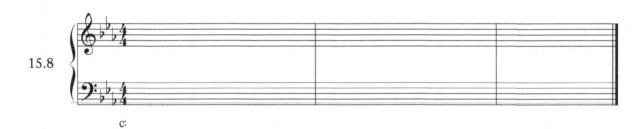

c:

15.9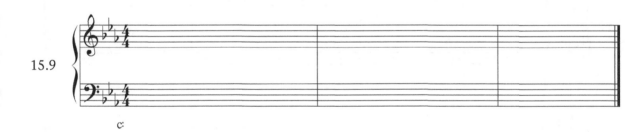

c:

15.10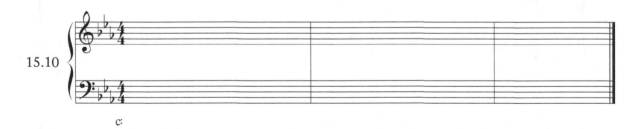

c:

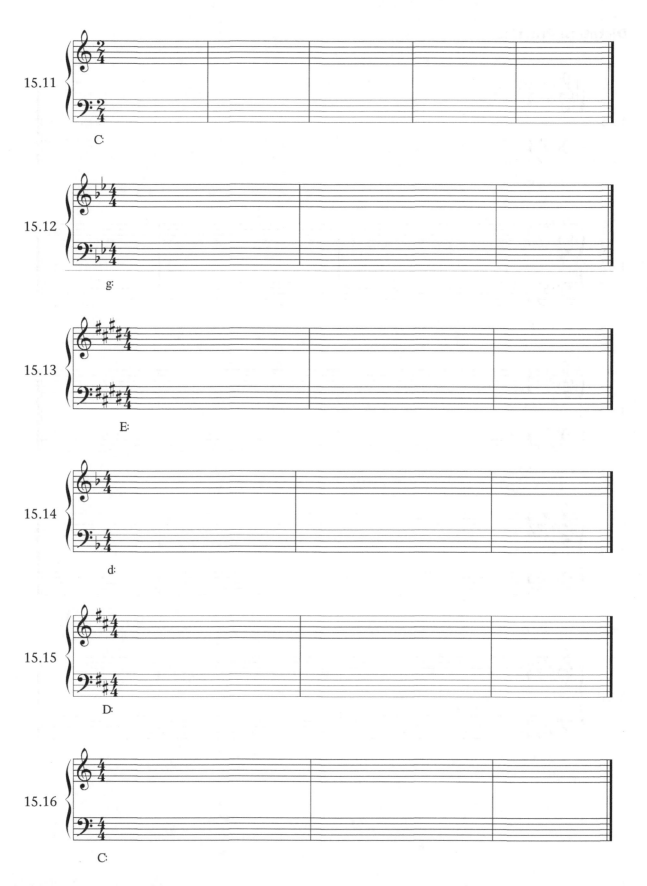

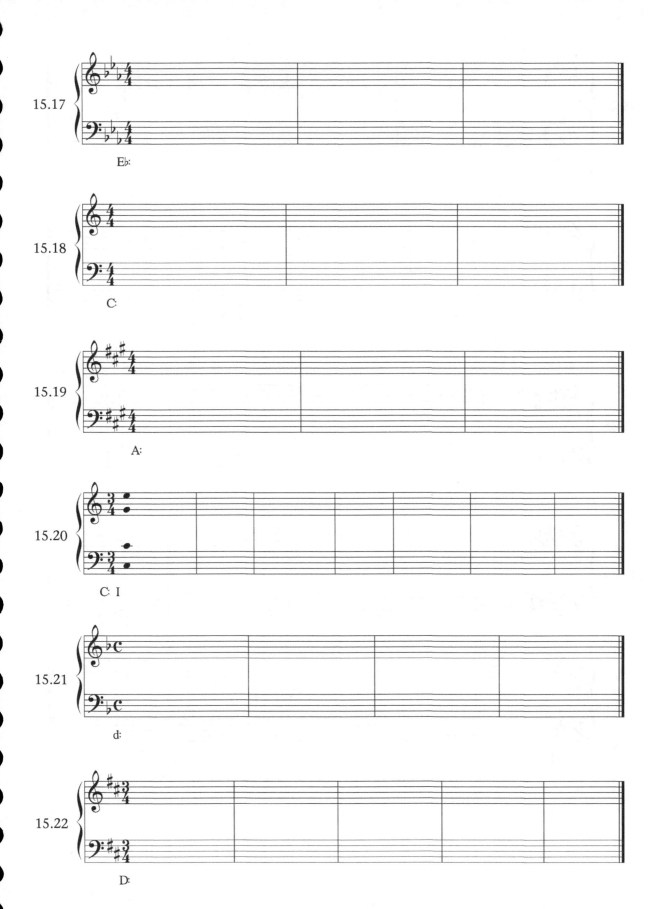

15.23

Bb:

15.24

g:

15.25

F: V⁷

15.26

c#:

15.27

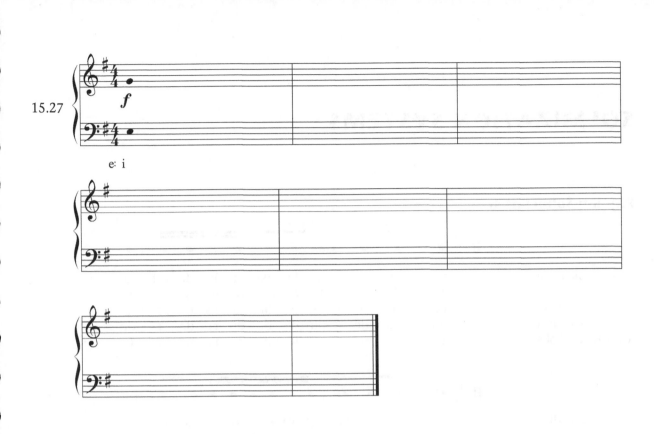

e: i

SOLMIZATION SYSTEMS

Rhythm Solmization

takadimi[1]	ta	ta	di	ta	ki	da	ta	ka	di	mi	ta
	1	2	&	1	&	a	2	e	&	a	1
Kodály[2]	ta	ti	ti	tri	o	la	ti	ka	ti	ka	ta
Gordon[3]	du	du	de	du	da	di	du	ta	de	ta	du
McHose & Tibbs[4]	1	2	te	1	la	li	2	ta	te	ta	1

takadimi	ta	ta	ki	da	ta	va	ki	di	da	ma ta	di	ta
	1	2	&	a	1	2	3	4	5	6 2	&	1
Kodály	ta	ti	ti	ti	ti	ka	ti	ka	ti	ka ti	ti	ta
Gordon	du	du	da	di	du	ta	da	ta	di	ta du	de	du
McHose & Tibbs	1	2	la	li	1	ta	la	ta	li	ta 2	te	1

Pitch Solmization

movable *do* solfège:	do	re	mi	fa	sol	la	ti	do
fixed *do* solfège:	re	mi	fa	sol	la	ti	do	re
scale degree numbers:	1	2	3	4	5	6	7	1

do	di	re	ri	mi	fa	fi	sol	si	la	li	ti	do
re	re	mi	mi	fa	sol	sol	la	la	ti	ti	do	re

do	ti	te	la	le	sol	se	fa	mi	me	re	ra	do
re	do	do	ti	ti	la	la	sol	fa	fa	mi	mi	re

1. Richard M. Hoffman, William L. Pelto, and John W. White, "Takadimi: A Beat-Oriented System of Rhythm Pedagogy," *Journal of Music Theory Pedagogy*, 10 (1996): 7–30.
2. Lois Choksy, *The Kodály Method: Comprehensive Music Education from Infant to Adult* (Englewood Cliffs, New Jersey: Prentice Hall, 1988), 14–16.
3. Edwin E. Gordon, *Rhythm: Contrasting the Implications of Audiation and Notation* (Chicago: GIA Publications, Inc., 2000), 98–104.
4. Allen McHose and Ruth Tibbs, *Sight-Singing Manual*, 3rd ed. (New York: Appleton-Century-Crofts, 1957), 6–9.

GLOSSARY OF MUSICAL TERMS

A piacere freely
Adagietto a little faster than adagio
Affettuoso affectionate, warm-hearted
Agitato agitated
Allegretto a little less fast than allegro
Allegrissimo very fast
Allegro fast
Amabile with love
Andante somewhat slow
Andantino a little faster than andante
Anima spirit
Animato animated
Animé animated
Appassionato impassioned
Assai extremely
Avec mouvement with motion
Ballando dancing
Berceuse lullaby
Bewegt agitated, somewhat fast
Breit broad, stately
Brillante brilliant, glittering
Brio verve
Calmo calm
Cantabile singing
Comodo at a comfortable pace
Con with
Deciso decisive
Deliberatamente deliberately
Dolce sweetly
Dolcissimo very sweetly
Dolente sorrowful
Doloroso sadly
Doux sweet, soft
Doux et expressif soft, expressive
Drammatico dramatic
Einfach simple
En allant flowing
Energico energetic
Eroica heroic
Espressivo expressive
Etwas somewhat
Expressif expressive
Fastoso pompous

Feierlich solemn
Feurig fiery
Fliessend flowing
Forza force
Fretta haste
Frisch brisk
Fröhlich light-hearted
Funèbre funereal
Fuoco fire
Gedehnt sustained
Gemütlich comfortable, pleasant
Geschwind quick
Getragen sustained
Giocoso playful
Gioviale jovial
Gracieux graceful
Grave slow
Grazioso graceful
Guisto precise
Gustoso amusing
Innig heartfelt
Innocente innocent
Kraft strength
Kräftig powerful
Langsam slow
Larghetto a little faster than largo
Largo slow
Lebhaft lively
Léger light
Lento a little faster than adagio
Lugubre mournful
Lunatico crazy
Lusingando coaxingly
Lustig merry
Maestoso majestic
Malincònico melancholy
Marcato accented
Marcia a march
Marziale martial
Mässig moderate
Mäßig moderately
Mesto sad
Misterioso mysterious

Moderato moderate
Modéré moderate
Molto much
Moto motion
Munter cheerful
Nobilmente nobly
Non troppo not too much
Pastorale pastoral
Patètico with great emotion
Pesante heavy
Piacevole graceful
Pomposo pompous
Presto very fast
Quasi almost
Rasch fast
Risoluto resolutely
Ritmico rhythmic
Ruhig calm
Scherzando jokingly

Schnell fast
Semplice simple
Sentimentale sentimental
Senza without
Sostenuto sustained
Spiritoso with spirit
Teneramente tenderly
Teneroso tenderness
Tranquillo tranquil
Trionfante triumphantly
Triste sad
Vif lively
Vite quickly
Vivace lively
Vivacissimo very lively
Vivement lively
Vivo lively
Zart tender, soft

Dictation Keys

PART 1

Rhythm

Module 1

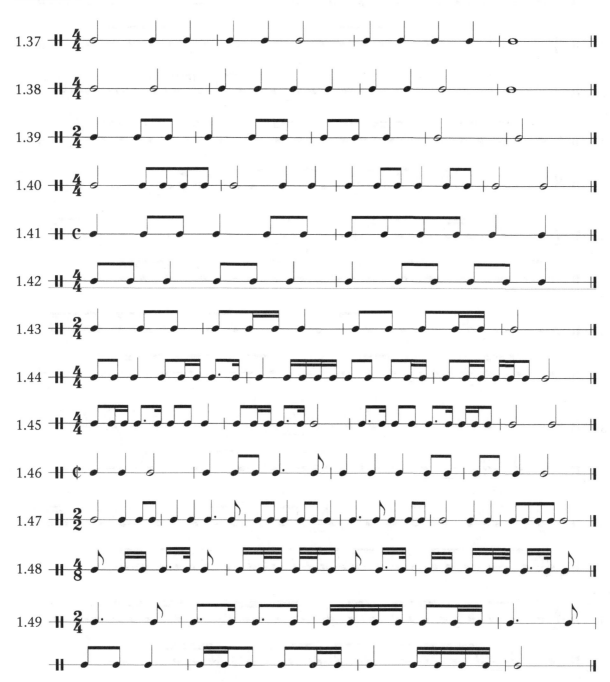

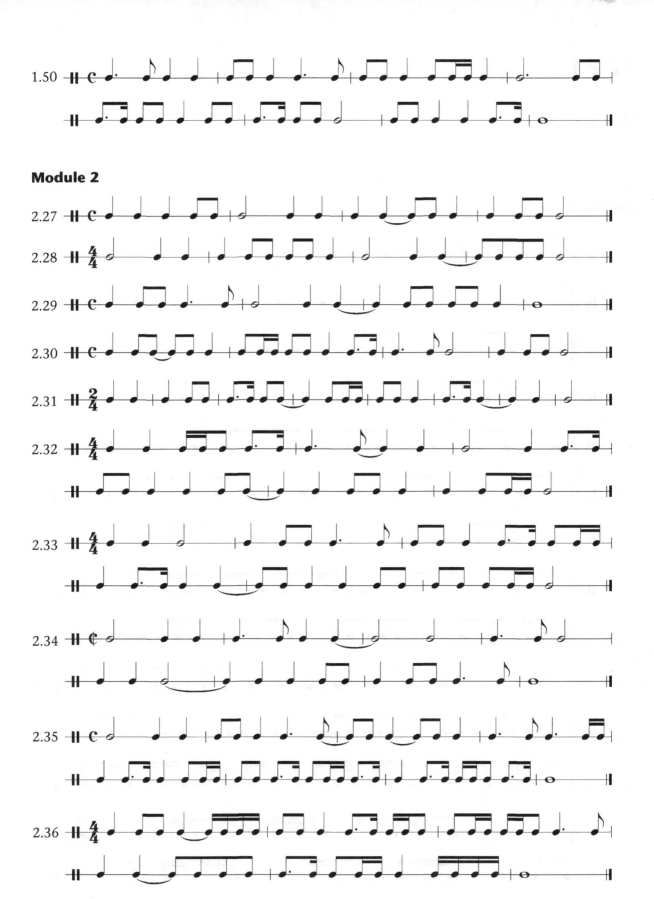

Module 2

Module 3

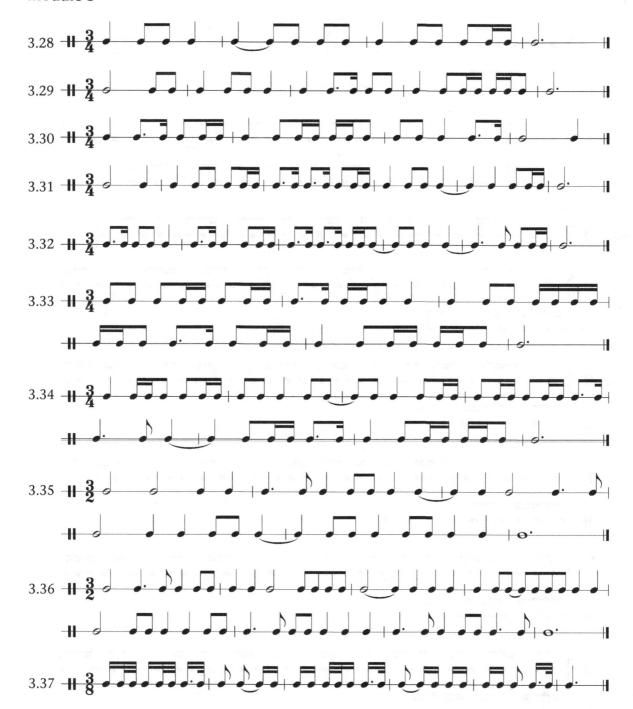

Module 4

Module 5

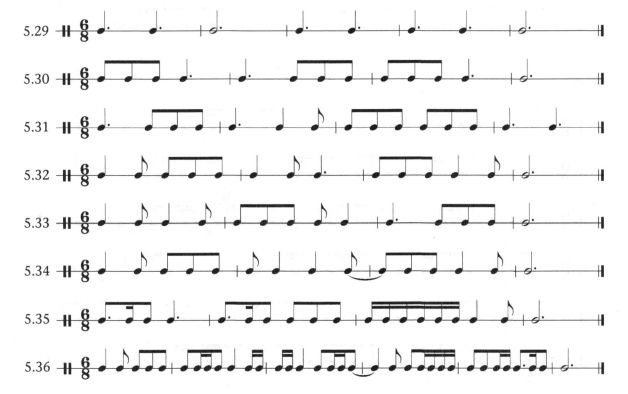

Module 6

Module 7

Module 8

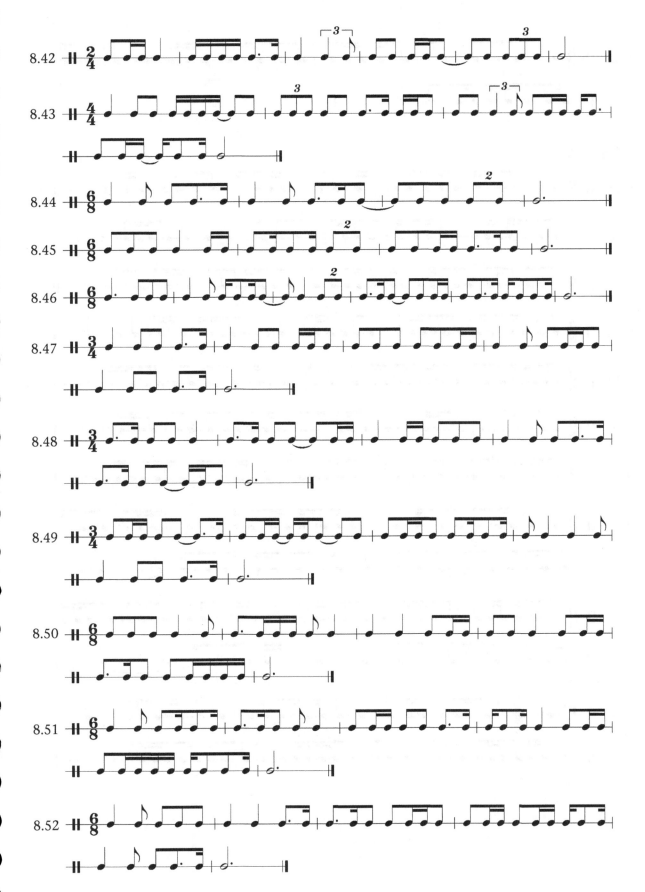

Module 9

Module 10

PART 2

Melody

Module 1

Module 2

Module 3

Module 4

Module 5

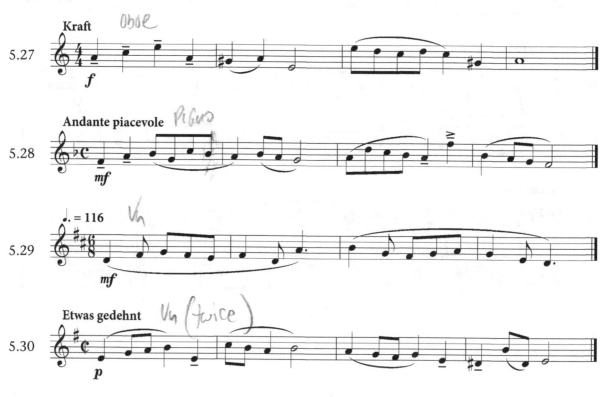

Module 6

6.36

Dolcissimo

6.37

Somber

6.38

Innocente

6.39

Module 7

Vivace

7.26

Moderato

7.27

7.40

Module 8

Berceuse

8.22

Doux

8.23

Breit

8.24

Amabile

8.25

Tempo comodo

8.26

Module 9

Module 10

Gemütlich

10.46

Fröhlich

10.47

Module 11

Mässig

11.18

♩ = 69

11.19

Adagio

11.20

♩ = 108

11.21

Marcia

11.22

Vivace

11.34

Module 12

Fliessend

12.40

mp

12.41

mf

Semplice

12.42

mp

Moderato

12.43

mf

Andante

12.44

mf < **f**

Maestoso

12.45

f

Marcia

12.46

f

Module 13

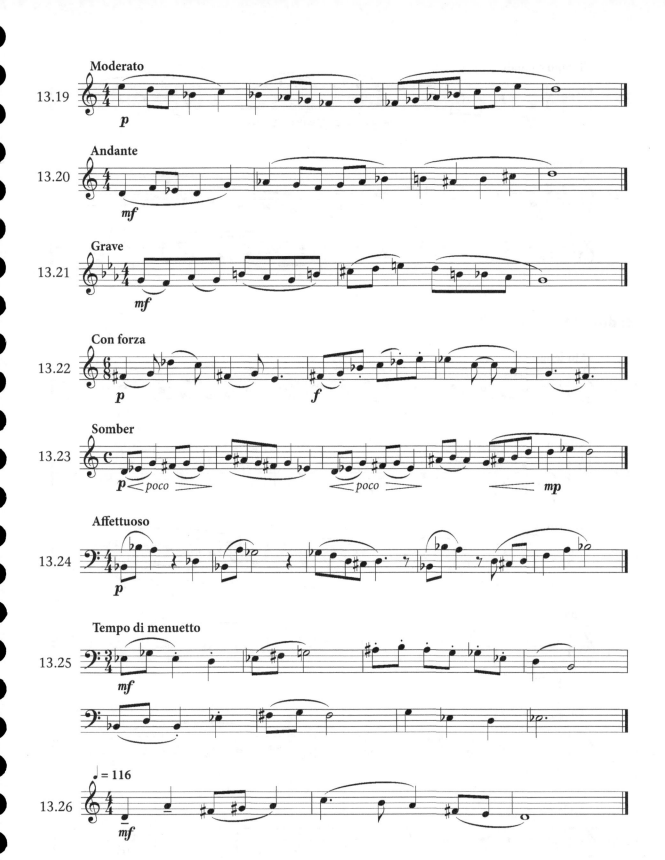

Module 14

PART 3

Harmony

1.6   B♭: I V I

1.7   B♭: I V I

1.8   G: I V_____

1.9   G: I V I

1.10   A: I____ V

1.11   G: I_____ V_____ I

1.12   d: i_____ V_____ i

1.13   g: i V_____ i V

1.14   B♭: V I_____ V I

1.15   C: V I I V I

1.16   e: V i V i V

Module 2

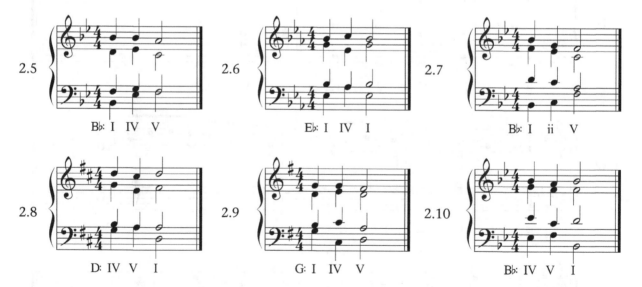

Module 3

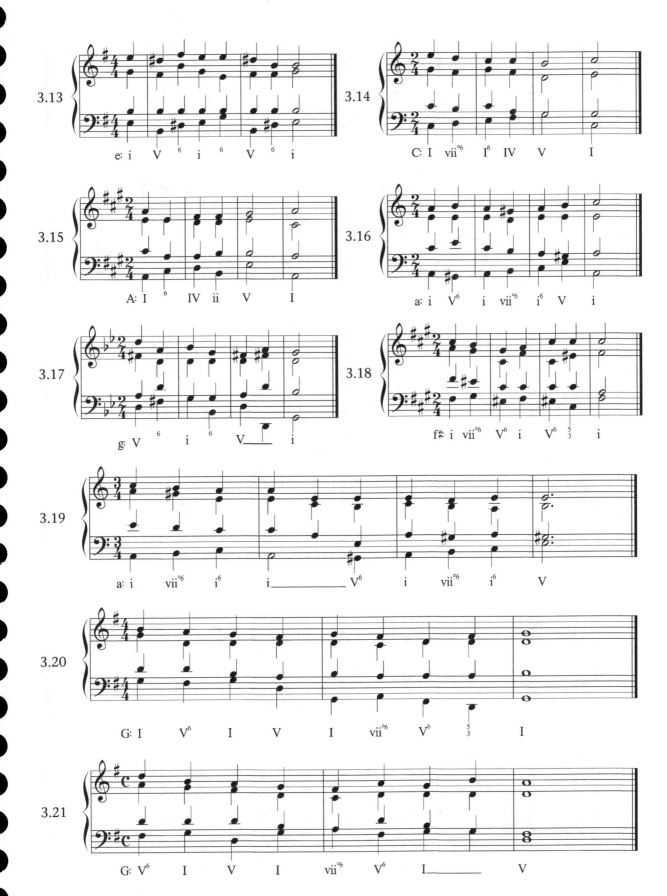

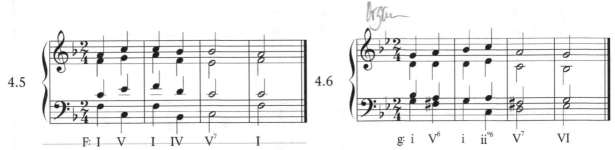

Module 4

Module 5

Module 6

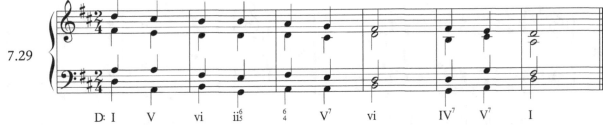

7.28

C: I   ii$^4_2$ V$^6_5$ I   I^6 V$^4_2$ I^6 $^5_3$ IV^7 ii$^{•6}_5$ $^6_4$ V^7 vi

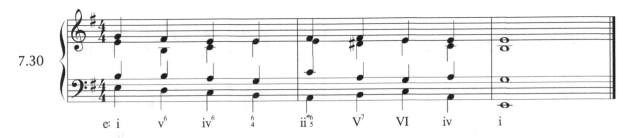

7.29

D: I   V   vi   ii$^{•6}_5$ $^6_4$ V^7 vi   IV^7 V^7 I

7.30

e: i   v^6 iv^6 $^6_4$ ii$^{•\#6}_5$ V^7 VI   iv   i

Tempo comodo

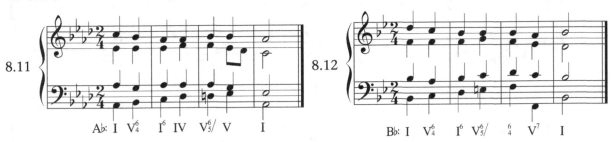

7.31

F: I   vi   iii   ii^6 V$^4_2$ I^6 V$^4_3$ $^6_5$ I

Module 8

8.11

A♭: I   V$^6_4$ I^6 IV   V$^6_5$/   V   I

8.12

B♭: I   V$^6_4$ I^6 V$^6_5$/ $^6_4$ V^7 I

8.41

d: i   6   iv   V⁷/   V   ⁴₂   i⁶   ii°⁶   V⁶₅/   V   i

Porta

8.42

f: i   vii°⁶   i⁶   V⁶₅   i   V⁶₅/

III   iv   ⁶₄   V⁷   VI   ii°⁶/

⁶₄   V⁷   i

Module 9

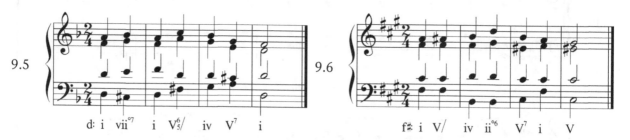

9.5

d: i   vii°⁷   i   V⁶₅/   iv   V⁷   i

9.6

f#: i   V/   iv   ii°⁶   V⁷   i   V

Module 10

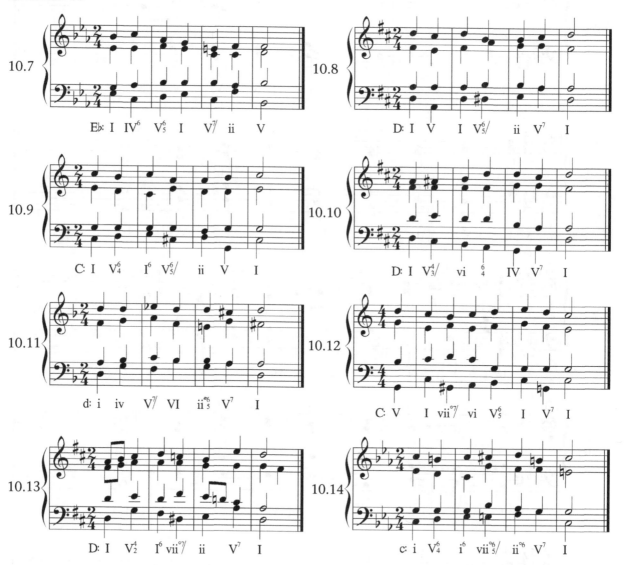

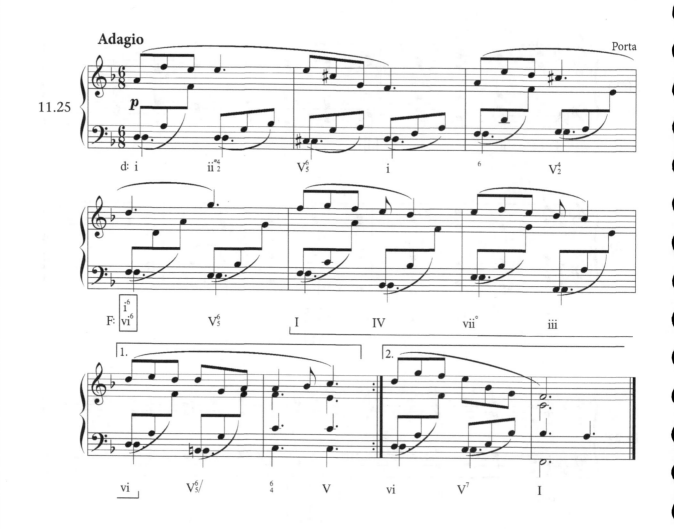

Module 12

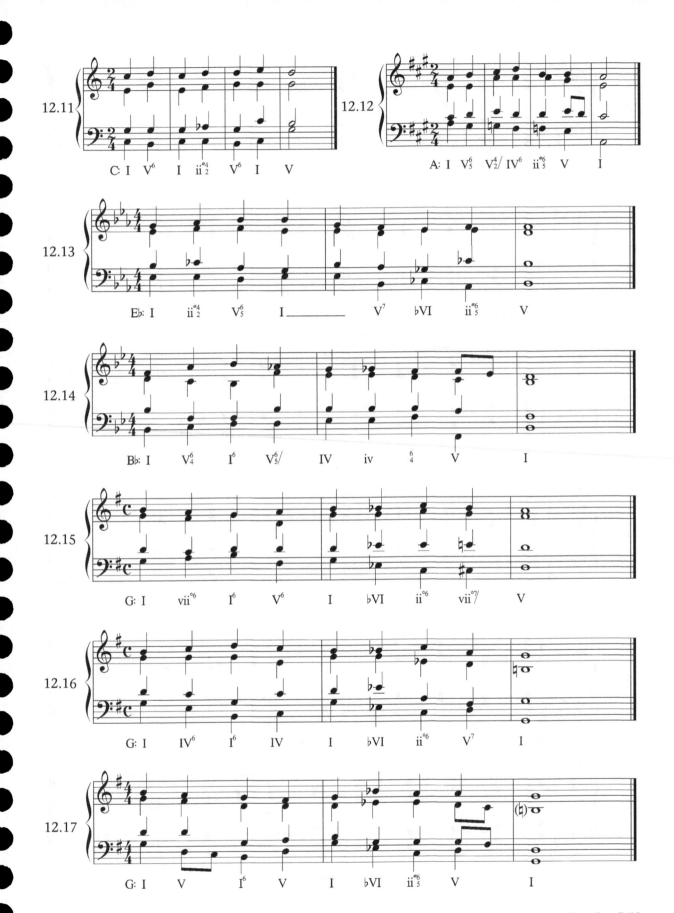

Module 13

13.4   d: i   V   i⁶   ♭II⁶ $^6_4$ V⁷   i

13.5   a: i   V$^4_2$ i⁶   VI   ♭II⁶   V   i

13.6   a: i   V$^4_2$ i⁶   V$^6_5$ i   ♭II⁶ $^6_4$ V⁷   i

13.7   g: i   V⁷   i   vii°⁶   i⁶   ♭II⁶   vii°⁷/   V⁷   i

13.8   d: i   iv   i   VI   i⁶   ♭II⁶ $^6_4$ V⁷   i

13.9   g: i   vii°⁷   i   vii°⁶   i⁶   ♭II⁶   vii°⁷/   V   i

13.10   d: i   VI   ♭II⁶   vii°⁷/   V⁷   i   vii°⁶   V$^6_5$ i

13.23

b: i   iv   VII   III   ♭II⁶   vii°⁷/ $^6_4$ V

i   v   VI   III   ♭II⁶   V⁷   I

Module 14

14.6

D: I   V⁶   I   IV⁶   It⁶   V   I

14.7

b: i   V   i   V$^4_2$ i⁶   It⁶   V

14.8

e: i   VI   iv   Ger$^{6+}_3$ $^6_4$ V⁷   i

14.9

d: i   V$^4_2$/   v⁶   It$^{6+}_3$ $^6_4$ ii°⁶   V

14.10

G: I   iv   V   vii°⁷/   vi   Fr$^{6+}_3$ $^6_4$ V⁷   I

Module 15

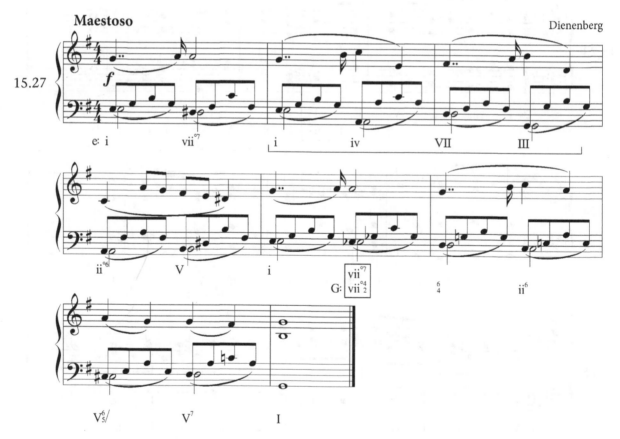